Turnaround Leadership

The Jossey-Bass Leadership Library in Education

Andy Hargreaves, Consulting Editor

The Jossey-Bass Leadership Library in Education is a distinctive series of original, accessible, and concise books designed to address some of the most important challenges facing educational leaders. The authors are respected thinkers in the field who bring practical wisdom and fresh insight to emerging and enduring issues in educational leadership. Packed with significant research, rich examples, and cutting-edge ideas, these books will help both novice and veteran leaders understand their practice more deeply and make schools better places to learn and work.

Andy Hargreaves is the Thomas More Brennan Chair in Education in the Lynch School of Education at Boston College and the author of numerous books on culture, change, and leadership in education.

For current and forthcoming titles in the series, please see the last pages of this book.

Michael Fullan

Turnaround Leadership

JOSSEY-BASS
A Wiley Imprint
www.josseybass.com

Published by Jossey-Bass
A Wiley Imprint
989 Market Street, San Francisco, CA 94103-1741   www.josseybass.com

Jossey-Bass books and products are available through most bookstores. To contact
Jossey-Bass directly call our Customer Care Department within the U.S. at 800-956-7739,
outside the U.S. at 317-572-3986, or fax 317-572-4002.

Jossey-Bass also publishes its books in a variety of electronic formats. Some content that
appears in print may not be available in electronic books.

Library of Congress Cataloging-in-Publication Data

Fullan, Michael.
    Turnaround leadership / by Michael Fullan.—1st ed.
        p.   cm.—(The Jossey-Bass education series)
    Includes bibliographical references and index.
    ISBN-13: 978-0-7879-6985-1 (alk. paper)
    ISBN-10: 0-7879-6985-0 (alk. paper)
    1. School management and organization.   2. Educational leadership.   3. Educational
change.   4. Educational sociology.   I. Title.   II. Series.
    LB2805.F85 2006
    371.2—dc22   2006010554

Printed in the United States of America
FIRST EDITION
PB Printing   10 9 8 7 6 5 4 3 2

Contents

Preface

My colleague and friend Sir Michael Barber was the chief architect
of the ambitious National Literary and Numeracy Strategy in England
during the 1997–2001 period. It was a strategy that saw eleven-year-
olds move from 62 percent proficiency on the average to some 75 percent, all within one election period. Michael was rewarded for his
efforts by being appointed in 2001 to create and lead a new unit
reporting directly to Prime Minister Tony Blair. The new entity was
called the Prime Minister's Delivery Unit (PMDU).

The role of PMDU was to monitor and stimulate ongoing improvement with respect to the prime minister's key priorities in the
four policy areas of health, education, transportation, and criminal
justice—quite a portfolio! PMDU was charged with working with
the relevant ministerial departments to improve performance relative to the policy goals set forth by Blair's government. PMDU has
four categories of performance: awful, adequate, good, and great.

We won't go into the details here of the fascinating story of how
many of the change strategies originally developed in education
shaped strategies in the other domains (for example, to improve
wait times in hospital emergency departments, increase the on-time
performance of trains, and reduce street crime in London). But
strategies adapted from education were used to establish specific and
rapid feedback data on performance linked to particular corrective
action, which in turn resulted in improvements. Trains are a huge

part of the English transportation system. On some reliability indi-cators, performance went from awful to adequate.

Michael Barber notes that there was nothing to be gained polit-ically by announcing proudly to the public that we have improved our train service from awful to adequate. If anything, there was a net loss in public trust because of course the public thought the ser-vice should be more than adequate in the first place.

This is my feeling about turnaround schools. They represent, at best, moving from awful to adequate, with no staying power to con-tinue to improve. Almost every developed country has specific pro-visions for intervening in situations of persistent poor performance. Variously called failing schools, underperforming schools, schools fac-ing challenging circumstances, schools in need of special measures, the terms all represent situations calling for action to "turn around" the school in question. In this book, I argue that the turnaround phe-nomenon is a dangerously narrow and underconceptualized strategy. We need, in other words, to cast the problem of failing schools in much larger perspective, not only in the context of the entire educa-tional system but in reference to societal development as a whole.

The issue is not moving from awful to adequate; nor is adequate to good good enough. We are finally at the stage where education for all does not have to be just a political slogan. *Turnaround Lead-ership* recasts leadership as part and parcel of a system transforma-tion. As Jim Collins observed, good is the enemy of great, and great is what we need.

Fortunately there is significant action on what I have come to call the trilevel solution: developing new capacities needed to re-form the entire system within and across the three levels of school and community, district, and state (Fullan, 2005; Fullan, Hill, and Crévola, 2006).

I am especially honored to be writing a book in a series organized by Andy Hargreaves. Hargreaves and Fink's book (2006) on *Sustain-able Leadership* is a relentless and compelling attack on the narrow-ness of strategies such as "turnaround schools," and offers a powerful set of seven interlocking principles of sustainability. I also would like to thank Andy for his incisive feedback on this book.

In our most recent book, *Breakthrough,* my coauthors, Peter Hill and Carmel Crévola, influenced my thinking in deep ways as we developed an on-the-ground case for improving *all* elementary schools.

Michael Barber continues to be an inspiration as we explore situations of system transformation in several countries around the world. Michael is one of the best system thinkers in action on the planet. My thanks also to the "saint," Clif St. Germain, for his initiative and partnership in writing our recent field guide to help schools become *Learning Places*.

I have a special regard these days for Ontario because Premier Dalton McGuinty; the former Minister of Education, Gerard Kennedy (who recently left his portfolio to pursue the federal Liberal leadership post); and the new Minister of Education, Sandra Pupatello, have invited me to help design and implement a systemwide reform that focuses on all four thousand elementary schools in all seventy-two districts in the province. Working with the deputy minister, Ben Levin, and the head of the newly formed Literacy and Numeracy Secretariat, Avis Glaze, we have assembled a fantastic joint effort, which involves partnerships aomng districts, schools, administrators, teacher unions, trustees, parent groups, other agencies, and the government. The Ontario school system can be classified as good by most world standards, but it is not great. There are schools that are awful or adequate—not by their own doing, but because the system has not invested in their development until recently. We have already made significant progress in two years. The next two years should be revealing as we attempt to go deeper and deeper, in partnership with schools and districts across the province.

I thank Claudia Cuttress, who for more than a decade has been the mainstay of support and development of materials behind the books and our consulting and capacity building work around the world.

My thanks also to my friend Betty Walters, who produced the manuscript burning the midnight oil.

Finally, it gives me great pleasure to acknowledge the countless colleagues around the world—practitioners, policymakers, and academics—with whom I have had the pleasure of working on issues of the utmost societal importance. My friends, we are finally getting somewhere. We know what needs to be done, and much of it is under way. I dedicate this book to making turnaround more than the latest strategy, so that we can get on with the deeper transformation so badly needed in our public school systems.

About the Author

Michael Fullan is professor of policy studies at the Ontario Institute for Studies in Education of the University of Toronto. Recognized as an international authority on educational reform, he is engaged in training, consulting, and evaluating change projects around the world. His ideas for managing change are used in many countries, and his books have been published in many languages.

Fullan led the evaluation team that conducted a four-year assessment of the National Literacy and Numeracy Strategy in England from 1998 to 2002. In April 2004, he was appointed special advisor to the premier and the minister of education in Ontario. His widely acclaimed books, translated into many languages, include *Leading in a Culture of Change*, the *What's Worth Fighting For* trilogy (with Andy Hargreaves), the *Change Forces* trilogy, *The New Meaning of Educational Change* (Third Edition), *The Moral Imperative of School Leadership, Leadership and Sustainability: Systems Thinkers in Action, Breakthrough* (with Peter Hill and Carmel Crévola), and *Learning Places* (with Clif St. Germaine).

ONTARIO
PRINCIPALS'
COUNCIL
Exemplary Leadership
in Public Education

The Ontario Principals' Council is a voluntary professional association for principals and vice-principals in Ontario's public education system. We believe that exemplary leadership results in outstanding schools and improved student achievement. To this end, we foster quality leadership through world-class professional services and supports. Through our ISO 9001 registered quality management system, the Ontario Principals' Council and its professional development division, Education Leadership Canada, strive to continuously achieve "quality leadership—our principal product."

Turnaround Leadership

1

The Real Reform Agenda

The real reform agenda is societal development. Not in an abstract sense, but empirically. Not in broad strokes, but through identifying precise themes and their consequences for better or for worse. Let us give the chapters one-word names, so that we can quickly and clearly see the flow of the argument. Chapter One is the Society Chapter. We will see the dynamics of what makes societies healthy or sick, and then insert the role of education. Sick education systems mirror sick societies, not only because they directly affect one another but also because the internal dynamics of diseased systems are similar.

The Turnaround Chapter is Chapter Two. Here we see played out in the education system many of the same processes that make societies sick. We identify some positive things that turnaround schools do to get off the critical list, going from bedridden to barely standing; and we identify what is needed for schools to become healthier all or most of the time.

Chapter Three is the Change Chapter. What motivates people in large numbers to change? It turns out that the answer is not so obvious. It is not a compelling, clear argument of long-term dire consequences that moves people to action. Environmentalists and early childhood educators have long argued in vain for immediate action in order to head off or reverse predictable and costly negative outcomes. Not even palpable, undesirable, gut-wrenching conditions of human misery attract forceful action, AIDS in Africa being a prime example. We need instead to draw more perceptively on what motivates people to engage in change, and what mechanisms and dynamics represent change forces commensurate with the transformation required.

The final chapter is the System Chapter. Turning a system around builds on the ideas of the first three chapters in defining a way forward. When all is said and done, *Turnaround Schools* is about getting off the road to perdition, and on the road to precision. The road to precision is not one of prescription. It is a matter of being best equipped with capacities that increase the chances of being dynamically precise in the face of problems that are unpredictable in their timing and nature, largely because they arise from human motivation and interaction. The System Chapter focuses on the role of leadership, not the leader who can come into town and save a single school (temporarily) but leaders whose very actions change the systems they work in. System thinkers in action, as I call them, are conscious of the fact that they are changing contexts as they help solve problems within them. So, society, turnaround, change, and systems: a unified set for addressing today's real reform agenda.

What Makes Societies Tick

Richard Wilkinson starts his book *The Impact of Inequality* with these words: "Within each of the developed countries, including the United States, average life expectancy is five, ten or even fifteen years shorter for people living in the poorest areas compared to those living in the richest" (2005, p. 1). I draw heavily here on Wilkinson's impressive synthesis of research on the impact of the gap between the poor and the rich. Interestingly, some of the deepest reasons for greater ill health among the poor in developed countries are not the obvious ones (such as exposure to physically unhealthy circumstances; but see later my discussion of Berliner's analysis [2005]). Wilkinson found that the main reasons, like many aspects of change, are sociopsychological, arising from not so much the circumstances in which we find ourselves but how we experience or perceive our daily lives in such circumstances. As Wilkinson describes:

> The biology of how psychological factors affect health seems to hinge predominantly on the extent to which they cause frequent or recurrent stress. Chronic stress affects numerous physiological systems, including the cardiovascular and immune systems, increasing our vulnerability to a very wide range of diseases and health conditions. . . .
>
> Because psychological factors influence health through stress, the main psychosocial factors identified by research are also likely to be the most important sources and symptoms of chronic stress in modern societies. They include depression, anxiety, helplessness, hostility, insecurity, and lack of a sense of control—not to mention the pressures that lead people to dependency on prescribed or recreational drugs. . . .
>
> On the positive side, feeling happy and in control of life, having friends, and enjoying good relationships all seem highly beneficial to health [2005, pp. 12–13].

In other words, the social meaning of people's circumstances have profound consequences: "Inequality promotes strategies that are more self-interested, less affiliative, often highly antisocial, more stressful, and likely to give rise to higher levels of violence, poorer community relations, and worse health. In contrast, the less unequal societies tend to be much more affiliative, less violent, more supportive and inclusive, and marked by better health" (Wilkinson, 2005, p. 23).

Wilkinson demonstrates that the core problem in most developed countries is not low material living conditions per se but rather low social status, which has corrosive social consequences "such as feeling looked down on, having an inferior position in the social hierarchy, and subordination (and therefore also a reduced ability to control one's circumstances and work)" (p. 25).

Thus the quality of social relations is better in more equal societies, where "people are much more likely to trust each other, [and] measures of social capital and social cohesion show that community life is stronger, and homicide rates and levels of violence are consistently lower" (p. 33).

Wilkinson presents data indicating that the United States trails behind most developed countries in life expectancy despite its wealth and high expenditure on medicine. The reason: "U.S. income differences are the widest of any of the rich developed market democracies" (p. 40). This inverse relationship between income inequality and life expectancy holds for all main developed countries, with Japan and Sweden at the higher end of the scale and the United States at the lower end. Canada is closer to Japan and Sweden.

In examining income differences across countries, Wilkinson shows that living standards figure only when they are too low to furnish such basics as clean water and adequate nutrition. This is no longer the case for the vast majority of people in developed countries: "As countries get richer and fewer people go without basic necessities, the relationship between measures of average living standards (such as gross domestic product per capital) and health progressively weakens" (p. 67).

Among the richest countries "we find no relationship whatsoever between GDP and average life expectancy." Citing numerous studies, Wilkinson shows time and again that "low social cohesion and income inequality [as distinct from average income] are at the top of the list of explanations for the decline of life expectancy" (p. 118).

The smaller the income gap, the greater the social capital or cohesion, and vice versa. In examining economic trends in several countries over time as they relate to incidents of violence, Wilkinson concludes: "There can be no doubt of the direction of causality, namely, that as economic disruption and dislocation widens, income differences lead to the deterioration of the social fabric and the rise of violence" (p. 207).

The lack of social cohesion in the more unequal societies has multifaceted negative consequences, notably the tendency in "societies with bigger inequalities to show more discrimination against vulnerable groups, whether women, religious or ethnic minorities" (p. 28), which "is part of a wider process of downward discrimination in which people who feel humiliated try to repair their sense of selfhood by demonstrating their superiority over more vulnerable groups" (p. 219). When inequality is high, anxiety and insecurity take their toll even if one is not aware of them. (The biological pathways in which recurrent stress affects health are hidden from one's conscious self.)

Wilkinson's main conclusion is that getting richer, whether as an individual or as measured by average country income (as with GDP), has little to do with happiness. He quotes Frank (1999, p. 111): "Study after careful study shows that beyond some point, the average happiness within a country is completely unaffected by increases in its average income level."

In pursuing self-interested economic development, Wilkinson predicts that we will create (indeed, we are creating) "a misunderstood and unhappy version of the humanity we plan for" (p. 263). Wilkinson then concludes that we "fail to recognize that what really matters to us, the source of our real satisfaction or dissatisfaction, just like the main sources of our stress and unhappiness, is to be found in the quality of social relations" (p. 263).

So why should the rich care? This is a complex question to answer, and some of the exploration must be speculative, because the very rich of course do not overtly discriminate (who was it that said, "What I like about snobs is that they leave you alone"?). Wilkinson's analysis was not based just on the rich and poor ends of the social scale; rather, his argument is that inequality negatively affects the entire distribution across the whole scale.

It seems to me that there are three main reasons we should all care about the solution, which is to raise the economic bar as we close the income gap. It is possible for individuals to hold any two or all three reasons (being multimotivated is not unusual). The reasons are social justice, health and well-being, and economic development. No one reason is likely to carry the day, but a deeper insight into how all three function in concert may have broad appeal.

The social injustice or moral purpose argument is palpable. Its major appeal is not just because of the obvious visible suffering and misery caused by inequality but how Wilkinson's analysis helps us see the mechanisms through which stress and deterioration versus happiness and growth operate. It is not just the social justice value we can endorse: we can actually envisage new processes through which major societal development (with multifaceted benefits) can occur. Social justice has always been a motivator for some. We must find a place for social justice where many can be attracted to the value of making society more beneficial to the vast majority of citizens.

Health and well-being, as we have seen through Wilkinson's analysis, is another reason for concern. The social costs for everyone in societies that are unequal are seriously on the rise. Remember: we are not talking only about historically poor countries, but also about how the richer an unequal society gets the worse off it becomes. There is a limit to this trend. Perhaps the relatively richer also have or will have lower life expectancy in unequal societies than their counterparts in more equal ones because of the prolonged stress of living in a society with ever less social cohesion. It is not hard to imagine that in the long run the growing social tensions in progressively unequal societies will challenge democracy itself. In short, a political case—that is, to maintain the legitimacy of the people—can be made for being concerned with a growing income gap within a given country.

The economic argument is the trickiest. The United States has become incredibly wealthy as a nation while becoming more unequal. But again, there is a limit. The debt in the United States is now in the trillions of dollars. In the long run, a healthier economy depends on the labor productivity of all its citizens, not just some. There is no question that the social consequences embedded in Wilkinson's analysis will have a growing adverse effect on the economy.

We are now nudging closer to the education system. Labor productivity is related to level of education. In a recent analysis by the C. D. Howe Institute of Canada, Coulombe and Tremblay (2005) drew this powerful conclusion: "A country's literacy scores rising by 1 percent relative to the international average is associated with an eventual 2.5 percent relative rise in labour productivity and a 1.5 percent rise in GDP per head. These effects are three times as great as for investment in physical capital. Moreover, the results indicate that raising literacy and numeracy scores for people at the bottom of the skills distribution is more important to economic growth than producing more highly skilled graduates" (p. 8).

The authors go on to say that "making the overall labour force more productive" generates greater economic payoff, "as opposed to developing highly talented individuals who may, among other things, have a positive impact on growth through their contribution to innovation and technological progress" (p. 10). The point is not that one has to choose between the two but rather that investment in the former, making the overall labor force more productive, is essential. If we link Coulombe and Tremblay's finding to Wilkinson's deeper analysis of the sociopsychological links to stress and well-being, the payoff for individuals and for society becomes manifold. Reducing the gap as you raise the economic bar makes economic sense.

In sum, the real reform agenda is raising the income bar while closing the gap between the richest and the poorest. Social justice, health and well-being, and economic development all figure in the individual and societal benefits for the vast majority of societal members, not just the poor.

In this book, we are concerned with the contribution of education to gap closing. Other social policy areas such as inequality in the workplace, investment in housing and welfare, investment in skill development of adults, and combating racism are beyond our scope. Rothstein (2002), for example, argues that "any reasonable strategy to enhance economic well-being must include a balanced focus on schools as well as other institutions" (for example, fiscal, monetary, trade, and labor market policies; p. 1; see also Rothstein, 2004).

Wilkinson's findings are reinforced by another economist, James Heckman, in his analysis (2006) of the consequences of failing to invest in the development of disadvantaged preschool children. From examining a range of data he draws this conclusion: "Early interventions for disadvantaged children promote schooling, raise the quality of the workforce, enhance the productivity of schools, and reduce crime, teenage pregnancy, and welfare dependency. They raise earnings and promote social attachment. Focusing only on earnings gains, return to dollars invested is as high as 15–17 percent" (p. 2).

We are talking about hard-nosed economists who are essentially saying that improving education for all from day one, and raising the bar and closing the gap, has a double payoff for society, namely, economic prosperity and social cohesion. Heckman presents his argument in a nutshell:

1. Life cycle formation is a dynamic process where early inputs greatly affect the productivity of later inputs in the life cycle of children. Skill begets skill; motivation begets motivation. Early failure begets later failure.

2. Major economic and social problems can be traced to low levels of ability in the population.

3. Much public policy focuses on cognitive ability, and especially IQ.

4. Noncognitive skills are also important for success in life.

5. Motivation, perseverance, and tenacity feed into performance in society at large and even affect scores on achievement tests.

6. Early family environment is a major predictor of both cognitive and noncognitive abilities.

7. The previous point is a major source of concern because the family environment in the United States has deteriorated in the past forty years.

8. Early interventions promote schooling, reduce crime, enhance workforce productivity, and reduce teenage pregnancy.

9. These benefits have high benefit-cost ratios and rates of return.

10. Early interventions targeted toward disadvantaged children have much higher returns than later interventions such as reduced pupil-teacher ratios, public job training, convict rehabilitation programs, tuition subsidies, or expenditure on police [adapted from Heckman, 2006, pp. 3–4].

Heckman offers reams of evidence to back up his conclusions. Thus the first main point I have tried to establish is that we must view educational improvement in the larger context of its contribution to society. This is not, as we have seen, an abstract argument. There are specific mechanisms and consequences at work, and to understand them is to go far beyond the turnaround school problem.

The larger agenda is to tackle raising the bar and closing the gap in income and social status in society. Failure to address this as the core goal results in greater violence. Even in Toronto, with its reputation as "the good and the clean" city embracing ethnic diversity, a spate of gun violence has erupted recently. Toronto has the greatest income differential of any city in Canada.

The solutions are not simple, but my argument is straightforward. First, focus on the societal problem of income differential and employ direct community-based short-term and long-term strategies. Second, conceive of education as playing a role in gap closing, especially as we shall see by working intensely on the three basics of literacy, numeracy, and what I will call the well-being of students (a term that encompasses emotional intelligence, character education, and safe schools).

What Makes Education Tick

It should come as no surprise that the size of the gap in education performance parallels the income gap country by country. That is, countries with larger education gaps are also those with higher income differentials. We are talking here only about developed countries. The Organization for Economic Cooperation and Development (OECD) monitors the performance of economic and social indicators over time for its thirty-two member countries, the richest countries in the world. One of OECD's main ongoing projects is the Programme for International Student Assessment (PISA). The PISA 2001 tests in literacy were given to more than 250,000 fifteen-year-old students in the thirty-two countries. As examples, in terms of mean or average literacy scores Finland performed best, Canada was near the top, the United States smack in the middle, and Mexico and Brazil at the bottom.

PISA also examined the reading scores of the 25 percent of the students with the lowest-ranked parental occupations as compared to the 25 percent with the highest-ranked occupations (this is a proxy measure for the size of the economic differences in the country). When this analysis was done, the United States, which had ranked fifteenth in the mean score comparison, dropped to twenty-third. In other words, the greater the economic differential the greater the gap in reading scores. Similar detailed analysis is now being conducted on the 2003 math assessment, which no doubt will show similar patterns.

We find further confirmatory evidence of the patterns being discussed here in Doug Willms's national longitudinal study in Canada of "vulnerable children" (2003). Willms and his colleagues developed an index of vulnerability based on the degree of emotional and behavioral disorders evident in young children. It was already known that children with such characteristics have a statistically reduced chance of leading healthy and productive lives.

One of the surprising findings in Willms's study is that the relationship between childhood vulnerability and family income was not as strong as previously believed. True, the percentage of vulnerable children in the lowest quartile (measured by family income) was a high 37 percent, but the other three quartiles were also high (28 percent, 25 percent, and 24 percent respectively for lower-middle, upper-middle, and highest quartiles). This is another reason society and schools should be concerned with improvement for all.

A second important finding concerns what Willms calls "the hypothesis of double jeopardy":

> This hypothesis holds that children in low SES [socio-economic status] families are more likely to be vulnerable, but children from low SES families who also live in low SES communities are especially vulnerable. . . .
>
> A number of studies have found that children with average SES tend to have better outcomes if they attend a school with high average SES. Thus, the "context" of the school has an effect on a child's outcomes, over and above the effects associated with the child's individual family background. The contextual effect—the benefit associated with attending a high SES school—is generally attributed to positive peer interactions, parental involvement, high expectations of school staff and parents, and a positive disciplinary climate in the school. Moreover, there is some indication that this effect is particularly pronounced for children from low SES families, and thus we refer to this hypothesis as the hypothesis of double jeopardy [2003, p. 32].

The temporary point for our purposes is not that we should shuffle children around on the basis of SES, but that the quality of relations constitute the core characteristics of success. You do not get such quality in highly unequal societies.

David Berliner's brilliant analysis (2005) of the deadly impact of poverty in the United States makes a compelling case for why we must put school reform in societal context. Berliner first shows that the United States has the highest rate of children living in poverty among twenty-six developed countries, with only Mexico having a higher rate. He also supplies evidence clearly showing that not only does the United States have the highest rate among industrialized countries of those who are "permanently poor" (14.5 percent, compared for example to Canada's 8.9 percent or France's 6.6 percent), but even more alarmingly it has the highest rate of people staying poor if they become suddenly poor. With respect to the latter, one study identified people "who have become impoverished once in a three-year time period, say through illness, divorce, child-birth or job loss" (p. 8). Several countries had high rates of temporary poorness, but these numbers receded more rapidly than in the United States. Says Berliner (2005, p. 9), "Unlike other wealthy countries, we have few mechanisms to get people out of poverty once they fall into it."

Berliner proceeds to interrelate poverty, race, and student achievement using, among several sources, the well-designed PISA studies assessing the performance of fifteen-year-olds in literacy, mathematics, and science. Overall, U.S. students are about at the average for all OECD countries. But the gap between highest and lowest is among the largest of all countries. In a revealing sub-analysis, Berliner displays the literacy scores by country but disaggregates the U.S. score into four categories: U.S. average, average for white students, average for Hispanics, and average for African Americans. The U.S. average, as I have said, is in the middle (a score of 499 on OECD's standardized measure). But for white students the score was 538, third only to Korea and Japan; Hispanics and African Americans scored at 449 and 445 respectively, which was ahead of only Luxembourg and Mexico among the twenty-seven countries compared. These comparisons were not based directly on poverty (except insofar as race and poverty are so closely linked), so the differences would be even more pronounced were poverty the main basis for comparison.

Berliner then takes us into territory explored by Wilkinson, as we saw earlier, except he applies it directly to education achievement. He asked how poverty affects achievement. In a word, the impact is multifold and pernicious. Citing a series of studies, Berliner presents the compelling case that poor environmental conditions suppress the normal development of academic intelligence. Poverty, and all that it entails, has direct health and indirect physiological and psychological consequences that inhibit the capacity to learn. Among these consequences are health issues, neighborhood deprivation (as when communities lack mentors), and other aspects of collective efficacy necessary to help those in difficulty.

All of this is to say that we must work with turnaround schools with a greater understanding of the social context and its consequences on mental and physical well-being. This is not a book on community and economic development, but the connection is clear. We need to work on simultaneously reducing the income gap and the education gap. Each can influence the other. We know that when poor people somehow beat the odds and achieve educationally, they do better on almost all the aspects we have been discussing. Berliner presents a series of studies showing that a rise in family income positively affects achievement. He sums up the point in these words: "As poor families went from poor to a lot less poor, for whatever reasons, their children's performance began to resemble that of the never poor children with whom they were matched" (Berliner, 2005, p. 25). So direct policies to raise income along with a better understanding of the context and dynamics of turnaround situations need to be combined.

Berliner does not talk directly about the function of gaps per se. He does note that families once poor whose family income increases "have more dignity and hope . . . than do families in more dire straits, where anxiety and despair are more common emotional reactions" (p. 28). We know from Wilkinson that the latter deals a double blow: it is directly harmful to be poor, and feeling looked down on adds insult to injury.

When it comes to schools themselves, it is interesting to speculate whether the kind of sociopsychological phenomena that occur when there is a high-income differential also operate in highly unequal education systems. What this means is that schools in highly unequal education systems experience a similar double whammy. First, there is the direct negative consequence of being in a low-performing school, where conditions are not conducive to achievement. Second, if Wilkinson is right there would be the indirect psychological consequences associated with (to quote Wilkinson again) "corrosive social consequences such as feeling looked down on, having an inferior position in the social hierarchy, and subordination" (2005, p. 25). Indeed, there is evidence from the turnaround schools research I cite in Chapter Two that indicates this is the case.

Attending a poor school in a school system with great disparity between the poorest and richest schools would compound any vulnerabilities that the child brings to the school in the first place (Berliner, 2005). There are also psychological effects of being perceived as, or feeling, inferior. Certainly one can imagine this for children and their parents, but I am suggesting that teachers in poor schools also suffer the same downtrodden consequences. We will see in Chapter Two that the negative emotional effects of being in a failing school mimic those discussed by Wilkinson for people in highly unequal societies who feel disrespected and unworthy.

There is one more disturbing parallel in education to Wilkinson's analysis. In the same way that once the basic necessities of life are met further increases in income are not associated with greater health, what if achieving literacy for all by age eleven was considered a basic necessity? Put another way, achieving literacy for all students is just a start from adequate to good, if you like. Much more would have to be done to ensure that raising the bar and closing the gap progresses through high school in all key areas of learning.

We have, then, many reasons for addressing inequality in schools. The goal is to raise the bar and close the gap. Closing the gap is crucial in the context of overall improvement for the system as a whole. We would do well to compare ourselves with countries that improved steadily in education performance while at the same time reducing the disparity between the lowest quartile of students or schools and the highest quartile.

As we have seen, this is not just a matter of education policy and practice but also of social and economic policies, all devoted to the same end: improving the social environment as the route to greater prosperity, economically as well as for our health and well-being. This puts education reform in perspective and allows us to start with turning around schools, not as an end in itself but rather as part of a more fundamental reform agenda.

2

Turning Schools Around

Virtually every developed country has a policy to address schools experiencing persistent failure. Intervention is inversely proportional to success, as they say. Failing schools, schools on probation, schools facing challenging circumstances, schools in special measures, and schools unable to demonstrate "adequate yearly progress" (AYP) all get the "turnaround treatment."

At first glance, it looks as if these strategies are doing some good. Starting in 1997, England was the first country to focus on identifying and taking action in relation to schools that were deemed failing. The number of schools labeled as in need of "special measures" declined by half between 1998 to 2005. Note that many jurisdictions (including England) are moving to a wider classification of "poor-performing" or "underperforming" schools, which includes "failing schools" (needing special measures) and those underperforming, whether in challenging or privileged circumstances (that is, they are underperforming relative to their peers). In England, the total number of these poor-performing schools in 2005 was about 3–4 percent of the total, although this does not include other primary schools that were not performing to their potential (National Audit Office, 2006). A special point here is that systems are moving (as they should) to focus on schools in privileged situations that appear to be performing well on the national or state average but that are in fact underperforming or stagnant compared to some of their similarly well-off counterparts. We call these the "cruising schools" (Stoll and Fink, 1998). In any case, the number of schools in various problematic categories in England has declined over the years since 1998, and we have to attribute this to the intervention actions taken.

Henry Minthrop's study (2004) of eleven schools in the high-stakes states of Maryland and Kentucky reports that in all schools there was some indication of increased effort as a result of external pressure and direction. In Ontario, the government's turnaround strategy has resulted in improvement in reading scores in the majority of schools involved in the first cohort (23 of 29 schools improved performance) and is now showing similar increases in the 115 or so schools involved (Pervin, 2005).

We also have a good idea of what key factors affect improvement in these situations of turnaround. The National Audit Office (2006) in England identified five main reasons for a school's falling below acceptable standards: ineffective leadership, weak governance (each school in England is managed by a local governors council), poor standards of teaching, lack of external support, and challenging circumstances. Ansell (2004) conducted a thorough review of the field and identified several factors associated with turnaround success:

- Engage people or organizations with expertise and experience in improving underperforming schools in challenging circumstances, to provide advice and guidance.

- Appoint a new head teacher if possible. This is the best way to bring about the rapid cultural change that is required.

- Select an experienced head teacher with a demonstrated capacity to improve schools of this nature. If this is not possible, select a head teacher with strong intrapersonal and interpersonal skills who will accept external support and team solutions.

- Conduct a thorough review to identify the school's key weaknesses and to devise strategies to correct them.

- Monitor the implementation of the plan carefully and hold regular reviews of progress.

- Be clear about everybody's role in the leadership team. Have clear behaviors, tasks and targets for all.

- Consider contracting external service providers to undertake specific tasks and functions, e.g., financial management, procedures for underperforming staff [Ansell, 2004, pp. 4–5].

Note the heavy preponderance of external input and direction, a point we will come back to shortly. Minthrop also indicates how control and focus can lead to initial improvements: "Management in some schools tightened up; educators paid closer attention to state assessments; support from instructional specialists or 'highly skilled educators' intensified; and the adoption of new programs, strategies, and projects accelerated. In this way a number of schools were able to remedy some inefficiencies and provide more structure to teachers than had previously been there. Considering rampant capacity deficits, they did it mainly through increasing control and standardization of teachers' classrooms" (2004, p. 150).

The National Audit Office's report (2006) in England identified four specific actions associated with successful turnaround: improving school leadership (two-thirds of schools that turned around changed their head teachers (principals), improving teaching standards through capacity building, better management of pupil behavior, and external assistance and support including collaboration with other schools. To foreshadow a key point to be brought up later, the report (p. 14) observes that "there is little evidence available about the performance of recovered schools in the longer term." Indeed, this is my main conclusion for refashioning a beyond-turnaround solution: current turnaround strategies, as we shall see, are too little and too late, work on only a small part of the problem, and unwittingly establish conditions that actually guarantee unsustainability.

For a dramatic example of turnaround in a failing high school, see the BBC film "Ahead of the Class," starring Julie Walters, based on the true story of how Lady Stubbs moved into St. George's comprehensive secondary school in London, England—a seriously failing school whose previous head had been murdered on the job, although not by a student (see also Stubbs's 2003 book containing her self-account). In the space of less than two years, Stubbs and two hand-picked deputies she brought with her turned the school from being on "special measures" (England's failing-schools label) to being assessed by the external inspection teams as "acceptable." She did it through strong, relentless control and discipline (for staff as well as for students) and a deep respect for the welfare of the students. Then she and her deputies left!

There are signs that many schools are being rescued from the critical list. So, what is the problem? The main problem in a nutshell (to go back to Michael Barber's classification I mentioned in the preface) is that we are (1) moving schools from awful to adequate, (2) using external direction and control to temporarily help the situation, and (3) violating just about every change rule we know as to how to go down the path of deeper, sustainable reform. There is, in other words, virtually no chance the approach will result in good, let alone great, schools. In this chapter, I look more precisely at why this is inevitably the case, and how the psychology of failure plays itself out as a direct result of the strategies currently being used. These insights can then be used to direct our attention to more promising approaches.

The Road to Perdition

Because our strategies produce at best temporary and superficial results while leaving the main problem—the gap between low- and high-performing schools—to become more pronounced, we really are going down the road to perdition. A careful analysis of the structural and sociopsychological forces at play reveals which current approaches to reform not only fail but make matters worse. This both reflects and contributes to societal deterioration. In other words, the plight of turnaround schools reflects and crystallizes the issues and choices that were so brilliantly uncovered by Wilkinson (2005), Heckman (2006), and Berliner (2005), as discussed in Chapter One.

Minthrop captures the pattern: initial focus on control, reduction of gross inefficiencies, and reversal of decline, but only initially. For the majority of schools, probation was not lasting and "had not spurred performance increases on the scale needed to lessen their tremendous performance lag " (p. 150). Minthrop observes that teachers have two options for escaping probation: "They can strive for increased test scores, or they can exit the school" (p. 155). Guess what option many of the better teachers chose?

> The pressures of probation—that is, the stigma of being labeled "low performing"; the threat of further, perhaps more severe sanctions; and the experience of increased control that comes with new planning requirements, audits, and so on—may make teachers in low-performing schools more susceptible to external directives and provide incentives to focus on the goals of the state accountability system and put more emphasis on raising test scores.
>
> But probation pressures may also cause anxiety and concern about professional reputation, perhaps leading to diminishing job satisfaction. Job satisfaction affects turnover and absenteeism, and rather than compelling workers to extend effort and instilling the will to high performance, pressures are sometimes avoided *with exit*, particularly where exit options are abundant, which they are for the more talented teachers [Minthrop, 2004, p. 5, my italics].

You know the old song, "How ya gonna keep 'em down on the farm after they've seen Paree?" Well this is, "How are you going to keep them down on the farm once they have seen the farm!"

This phenomenon is systematically reinforced by certain features in union contracts in many cities, according to the findings in five school districts studied by Levin, Mulhern, and Schunck (2005). They identify (1) vacancy policies, (2) staffing rules in union contracts favoring seniority, and (3) late budget timetables that produce four negative, unintended consequences:

1. "Urban schools are forced to hire large numbers of teachers they do not want and who may not be a good fit for the job and their school" (p. 5). In their study, 40 percent of school-level vacancies were filled by voluntary transfers or excessed teachers about whom schools had either no choice at all or limited choice.

2. Levin and colleagues found that "poor performers are passed around from school to school instead of being terminated" (p. 5).

3. "New teaching applicants, including the best, are lost to late hiring" (p. 6), as transfers and other adjustments have to be addressed first.

4. "Novice teachers are treated as expendable regardless of their contribution to their school" (p. 6).

Their conclusion is as obvious as it is damning for the situation faced by failing schools: "Taken together, these four effects significantly impede the efforts of urban schools to staff their classrooms effectively and sustain meaningful schoolwide improvements. Forced to take teachers who may either be poor performers or ill-suited to the specific school context and culture, prevented from hiring many of the best new teacher applicants, and unable to adequately protect teachers they hope to keep, urban schools cannot exert sufficient control over the most important school-based factor that influences student learning" (Levin, Mulhern, and Schunck, 2005, p. 6).

Back to Minthrop and his conclusion about the two accountability systems—Maryland and Kentucky—in his study. These accountability schemes

> largely failed to instill meaningful performance goals in
> educators in the studied schools on probation, and they
> failed even more miserably with the more active mem-
> bers of the profession. An incentive system that cannot
> appeal to the higher performing parts of the workplace
> is doomed to failure. The systems insufficiently tapped
> into teachers' personal sense of responsibility for perfor-
> mance. As a result, school improvement for the major-
> ity was mainly externally induced and directed, prodded
> by administrators, instructional specialists, external con-
> sultants, staff developers and so on whose activities were
> moderately fuelled by a common desire among teachers
> [who remained] to get rid of stigma and scrutiny and
> eased by a disposition to be compliant that the culture
> of high stakes fostered [Minthrop, 2004, pp. 147–148].

If there were ever a recipe for going from awful to adequate that virtually guarantees (that is, establishes the conditions for) not being
able to move further, this would be it.

A key theme in this book concerns how emotions are generated
by social conditions, and what role these emotions play in pre-
venting or fostering needed reform. Failing schools are, of course,
brimming with emotions, usually of the negative variety.

Andy Hargreaves is one of the leading writers about the much-
neglected topic of emotions and change. In his paper "Distinction
and Disgust: The Emotional Politics of School Failure," Hargreaves
(2004) takes us back to American sociologist Richard Sennett.
In *The Hidden Injuries of Class*, Sennett discusses working-class
men and women who are struggling in their lives. What they craved,

says Sennett, was dignity and respect. But what they repeatedly experienced was denial of dignity in their daily encounters with failure, frustration, and shame. Sennett concludes that "the possibility of failure is the most uncomfortable phenomenon in American life. There is no room for failure in our schemes of rewards" (Sennett and Cobb, 1973, p. 183). We also know from Wilkinson (in Chapter One) the profound physiological and social consequences of prolonged negative emotions. In turnaround schools, we can see how students and parents suffer from the stress of exposed failures. I am adding teachers to this list of casualties.

I need to interrupt the flow of this argument to make a crucial point. The irony of what I am saying is that the sponsors of turnaround strategies are motivated, shall we say, to correct the very problem I am talking about. The goal is presumably to get the schools, and the people who inhabit them, off the road to perdition and on the road to dignity and respect as a result of better performance. My point is not to question intent but rather to point out that the strategies are perversely flawed, in a way that can be specifically uncovered—silver bullets that wound.

Hargreaves and Fink (2006) take up the theme of failing schools in their new book, *Sustainable Leadership*. They call turnaround schemes quick-fix solutions: "Quick-fix changes to turn around failing schools often exhaust the teachers or the principal, and improvement efforts aren't sustained over time. The principal's success in a turnaround school may lead to his or her rapid promotion, but then result in regression among teachers who feel abandoned by their leader or relieved when the pressure is off" (p. 57).

Hargreaves and Fink also worry about the "how we are going to keep them down on the farm" problem: "Outstanding teachers and leaders are drawn toward the most exemplary or highest-profile institutions, and at the same time they are drained away from the rest. For every beacon or lighthouse school that attracts most of the local resources and attention, dozens of surrounding schools are treated more like outhouses—low status places where districts dump their difficult students and weaker staff members" (p. 145).

Thus the gap widens, and we already know the rampant negative effects of living with low status relative to your more privileged peers.

Rosabeth Moss Kanter (2004) pursues the issues of turnaround in a fascinating way in her book *Confidence: How Winning and Losing Streaks Begin and End*. Confidence, she says, consists of positive expectations for favorable outcomes: "Confidence influences the willingness to invest—to commit money, time, reputation, emotional energy, or other resources—or withhold or hedge investments" (p. 7). Underconfidence "leads people to underinvest, to underinnovate, and to assume that everything is stacked against them, so there's no point trying" (p. 8). Using examples from sports, business, and schools, Kanter shows how failure or success can be contagious, more like a trajectory than an episode. Hargreaves and Fink say that the policy rhetoric on failing schools is one of overconfidence, which leads people to simplistic solutions and subsequently to simplistic interpretations as to why schools don't improve or keep on improving.

Kanter also offers insight into why it is easier to move schools from awful to adequate than it is to keep going after initial improvement: "People who have put in long hours willingly during the crisis can start to relax a little, enjoy the success, and maybe figure that they're good enough, unless they get more motivation to keep getting better" (p. 66).

It is easier to lose than to win because losing does not take any effort. In losing situations Kanter identified nine pathologies working as a kind of emotional and behavioral chain reaction: "Communication decreases, criticism and blame increase, respect decreases, isolation increases, focus turns inward, rifts widen and inequities grow, initiative decreases, aspirations diminish, and negativity spreads" (pp. 97–98). Echoing Minthrop's finding, Kanter observes that "during the downward spiral, the most desirable executives left because they had other options" (p. 138).

Kanter warns of "the dangers of false recovery": "The turnaround leaders' agenda is daunting: endless problems to fix, unpopular decisions to make, skeptics to convert, and the need to secure investment before investors see any wins to attract them. . . . there are so many things that can go wrong. Turnarounds often proceed unevenly, in fits and starts, and are fraught with the danger of false recoveries that cannot be sustained because fundamentals have not been fixed" (p. 173).

With all this doom and gloom, with failure being a syndrome of forces with its own negative trajectory, and with direct outside intervention not furnishing the conditions for sustainable turnaround, what can be done that is constructive? In the rest of this chapter, I outline what I call a directional solution. Chapter Three doubles back to ensure that we know enough about change knowledge to guide us in moving in this new direction. Chapter Four restates the challenge of turnaround schools as one of turning around the whole system; it features examples of what this new solution looks like.

Getting off the Road to Perdition

Elmore (2004b) gets us started when he says there can be no effective external accountability unless there is also internal accountability: "It appears from early research that school systems that improve are those that have succeeded in getting people to *internalize* the expectations of standards-based accountability systems, and that they have managed this internalization largely through modeling commitment and focus using face-to-face relationships, not bureaucratic controls. The basic process at work here is *unlearning* the behaviors and normative codes that accompany loose coupling, and learning new behaviors and values that are associated with *collective responsibility* for teaching practice and student learning" (p. 82, my italics).

Elmore goes so far as to say that "internal accountability precedes external accountability and is a precondition for any process of improvement" (p. 114).

Schools do not "succeed" in responding to external cues or pressures unless they have their own internal system for reaching agreement evident in organization and pedagogy. . . . These schools have a clear, strong internal focus on issues of instruction, student learning and expectations for teacher and student performance. In academia we call this a strong internal accountability system. By this we mean that there is a high degree of alignment among individual teachers about what they can do and about their responsibility for the improvement of student learning. Such schools also have shared expectations among teachers, administrators and students about what constitutes good work and a set of processes for observing whether these expectations are being met [p. 14].

Thus expectations, individual responsibility to act, and accountability (monitoring, feedback, correction) are aligned and collectively held and reinforced. Elmore found that in the schools in his study operating with internal accountability "collective expectation gelled into highly interactive, relatively coherent informal and formal systems, by which teachers and administrators held each other accountable for their actions vis-à-vis students" (p. 193).

In these schools, teachers and administrators had the internal capacity to interact productively with the external accountability systems (testing, curriculum guidelines, and so forth) in which their schools operated.

Now we are getting somewhere, but there is a fundamental dilemma. There are overall very few schools that have well developed internal accountability systems, and it is precisely the turnaround schools that do not have this capacity. But this is the point, as tough as it is. If we do not do something to increase the internal capacity of turnaround (really, all) schools, we will spend the rest of our days mired in the awful-to-adequate stew of failed reform.

Many of us—Elmore, Minthrop, Hargreaves, Kanter, and I—are saying the same thing in relation to what must be done differently. We need to reframe our entire reform strategy so that it focuses relentlessly and deeply on capacity building and accountability—a difficult but, I believe, increasingly doable high-yield strategy.

We have already seen Elmore's formulation of internal accountability linked to external schemes, complete with examples of some schools that are doing it. I refer to the strategy as "capacity building with a focus on results" and will lay out examples of this work in Chapter Four. Briefly, capacity building involves any policy, strategy, or other action undertaken that enhances the collective efficacy of a group to raise the bar and close the gap of student learning for all students. Usually it consists of the development of three components in concert: new knowledge and competencies, new and enhanced resources, and new and deeper motivation and commitment to improve things—again, all played out collectively.

We also saw Minthrop (2004) identify the fatal flaw of turnaround policies in high-stakes states. These policies actually weakened internal capacity as they propped it up temporarily by expanding the presence of external consultants and new (externally introduced, but soon to leave) turnaround principals. If done with enough intensity, a tight system like this can squeeze out initial improvements, but it will not create any basis for going further.

Minthrop's remedy for what is needed is again virtually identical to ours: "Investment in school capacity is key for the success of probation policies. In our schools, level of school capacity is the factor that best explains individual and organizational responses to probation. Work motivation and commitment to stay were strongly related to principal leadership, collegiality and perceived skill of colleagues. We found these skills and talents in short supply across the studied schools" (p. 156).

In short supply! Indeed, the supply dwindled as the heavy-handed external pressure and control took their toll. Neither Minthrop nor I call for the absence of pressure but rather for pressure that actually works to help pave the way for longer-term capacity building. In Chapters Three and Four, I will talk about "positive pressure"—pressure that serves to stimulate ongoing improvement, pressure that is built into the interactive culture of peers, pressure with a purpose, pressure that follows capacity building instead of preceding it, and pressure that is seen as fair and reasonable in the specific circumstances at hand.

In a similar but deeper direction of sustainability, Hargreaves and Fink (2006) lay out a radical agenda for shaping the capacity of school systems to engage in continuous improvement. Their seven principles of sustainability in concert focus on sustainable leadership as the solution:

1. Depth (sustainable leadership matters)
2. Length (sustainable leadership lasts)
3. Breadth (sustainable leadership spreads)
4. Justice (sustainable leadership does no harm to and actively improves the surrounding environment)
5. Diversity (sustainable leadership promotes cohesive diversity)
6. Resourcefulness (sustainable leadership develops and does not deplete internal and human resources)
7. Conservation (sustainable leadership honors and learns from the best of the past to create an even better future; pp. 19–20)

Hargreaves and Fink also uncover the disturbing consequences of "succession planning." In one of their studies they were able to trace succession of leaders in eight schools across a thirty-year period. They conceptualized these events in a fourfold table organized according to whether there was "continuity or discontinuity" of direction, and whether the succession was "planned or unplanned."

One would imagine, for example, that if you have good things going the idea is to plan for succession that builds on this initial positive direction. In our own work, as we have seen time and again, it is not turnover of leadership that is the problem but rather discontinuity of good direction. The strategies used for turnaround schools, as we mentioned, do not include building on good new direction, even if the turnaround is initially positive. In Lady Stubbs's St. George's school (2003) the great work that moved the school from awful to adequate over a two-year period was led by the head and two deputies, one of whom was groomed for (and we might say was perfect for) keeping the continuity of good direction. He applied but was passed over for the position as Lady Stubbs's successor in favor of an external candidate who (of course) had no knowledge of the new and better culture that was emerging in the school.

A turnaround school is a prime candidate for planned discontinuity—that is, the need to discontinue awful performance and redirect the school positively. In the majority of schools identified by policy as needing turnaround, new external leadership is in fact one of the first steps taken. I agree that this is a necessary first step in many cases. What we have seen, however, is that the second step is not thought through: How do you go about establishing a series of successive leaders that represent continuity of the new good direction?

Hargreaves and Fink (2006) found that a lot of unplanned succession—whether continuous or not—was a matter of luck. More to the point of a turnaround situation, which needs planned discontinuity, Hargreaves and Fink identify several examples where the good new work is short-lived because of the lack of a plan to build on it. Specifically:

> Discontinuity, that is reversing a bad situation, needs to be pushed with steadfastness, over a long period of time, until it becomes the new continuity. While planned discontinuity can yield rapid results, its leadership needs time to consolidate the new culture, to embed it in the hearts and minds of everyone. Repeatedly, planned discontinuity was effective in shaking up the schools in our

study but not at making changes stick. For example, because of his quick and visible success Bill Andrews was lifted out of Stewart Heights too early, after less than three years, to take a promotion in the district office. Leaders of planned discontinuity in other schools were also transferred to struggling schools elsewhere long before their existing work had been completed. The result was a constant cycle of change throughout schools in the system but little lasting improvement in any one of them [p. 69].

It is not only that the existing leader needs more time to work on the new direction; more importantly, a culture of distributive leadership that grooms new leaders for the next phase must be established. Without this attention, as Hargreaves and Fink conclude, "Recent success is discontinued, improvement gains are eliminated, and continuity is reestablished with earlier, more mediocre patterns" (p. 71). The end result, says Hargreaves, is a "perpetual carousel" where schools may "move up and down with depressing regularity" (p. 71). Sometimes you can turn around so much that you are still facing the same direction!

Our capacity building with a focus on results fits perfectly with Kanter's turnaround solution (2004), which is framed around the three connected cornerstones of accountability, collaboration, and initiative.

- *Accountability.* People want to share information and take responsibility; they have nothing to hide. They seek feedback and self-improvement. Because they feel committed, they communicate more often and make higher-quality decisions. They set high aspirations and respect each other for meeting high standards. They avoid excess and try self-scrutiny before blaming others.
- *Collaboration.* People want to work together. Mutual attraction is high, interpersonal bonds are strong, and relationships

are multifaceted because people take the time to know one another in a variety of settings. People are willing to help others and give them a chance to excel. They feel a sense of belonging that makes them more amenable to taking direction from others.

• *Initiative*. People feel that what they do matters, that they can make a difference in outcomes, so they offer ideas and suggestions. Expectations of success produce the energy to put in extra effort to keep going under pressure. People take initiative, and initiative results in improvements and innovations [pp. 46–47].

These behaviors, says Kanter, are central to confidence because they feed motivation and morale. Kanter presents examples of turnaround that combine accountability, collaboration, and initiative from sports, business, and schools. As well, she describes examples of its opposite in which a downward spiral erodes confidence and lowers morale and effort. Kanter asks rhetorically, "What is the most powerful factor in losing streaks?"

"Is it individual pessimism, too many negative thoughts? Is it lack of communication, lack of discipline, inability to pull together as a team? Is it ineffective leaders who make poor decisions, blame rather than motivate, and disappear frequently leaving groups adrift and helpless? Is it lack of financial resources to invest in new initiatives, or just keep current ones going? Is it lack of support from sponsors, customers, fans, opinion leaders, or rule makers" (p. 140)?

Her answer: it is all of those. Kanter does, as I have said, describe examples of successful turnaround. This is not the place to delve into specific solutions—a topic which I take up in Chapters Three and Four. In this chapter we are establishing the new agenda. Essentially, it involves leadership that develops strategies for building capacity with a focus on results. It is hard at the beginning, but a turnaround crisis often rallies enough resources and directed leadership for initial improvement. Nevertheless, "one victory does not make a turnaround" (Kanter, 2004, p. 125), so it is even harder in the middle when continuity of good direction is crucial (with the immediate crisis lessened) for establishing the cultural capacity to keep on going from adequate to good on the road to greatness.

When all is said and done, we are talking about change—not just what changes should be made, but the much more challenging question of how to go about changing extremely difficult circumstances. We need to go back to some basics: Under what conditions do people become energized to put in the effort required? How do people change their minds and habits? What will keep them going? Finally, the big question: How can we go beyond a few exceptional examples of success to make continuous improvement a characteristic of the vast majority of the constituent parts of the whole system? Put another way, if many parts of the system are not changing for the better, you cannot make progress on reducing the gap between high and low performers, which, as I have said, is the real reform agenda.

It is time to return to the mysteries of how people and systems change.

3

Change

Take any hundred books on change, and they all boil down to one word: motivation. If you want more words, the holy grail of change is to know under what conditions hordes of people become motivated to change (because we are talking about whole-system reform). The answer is not as straightforward as we would like.

The Mysteries of Change

If people were given a literal choice of "change or die," do you think most people would choose change? If you said yes, think again. Deutschman (2005) writes, "What if a well-informed, trusted authority figure said you had to make difficult and enduring changes in the way you think and act, and if you didn't you would die soon." The scientifically studied odds that you would change, he writes, are nine to one against you. Medical research shows that 80 percent of the health care budget is consumed by five behavioral issues: smoking, drinking, eating, stress, and not enough exercise. Deutschman quotes Dr. Edward Miller, the dean of the medical school and the CEO of the hospital at John Hopkins University, who talks about patients with severe heart disease. Miller says, "If you look at people after coronary-artery bypass grafting, two years later, 90 percent of them have not changed their lifestyle. Even though they have a very bad disease and they know they should change their lifestyle, for whatever reason, they can't" (Deutschman, 2005, p. 2).

Deutschman then quotes John Kotter of the Harvard Business School as saying, "The central issue is never strategy or structure. [It] is always about changing the behavior of people." Then Deutschman observes: "The conventional wisdom says that crisis is a powerful motivator for change [think turnaround schools]. But severe heart disease is among the most serious of personal crises and it doesn't motivate—at least not nearly enough. Nor does giving people accurate analyses and factual information about their situations" (p. 2).

Later in this chapter I set down a combination of factors that increase the likelihood of change in difficult circumstances (such as a persistently failing school), but let's explore the problem and solution a little further. In turning to at least a directional solution, Kotter says, "behavior change happens mostly by speaking to people's feelings. . . . In highly successful change efforts, people find ways to help others see the problems or solutions in ways that influence emotions, not just thought" (p. 2). Deutschman then offers additional useful insights. Fear, as in fear of dying, turns out not to be a powerful motivator beyond an initial immediate effect. Similarly, in the United States the fear of not meeting "adequate yearly progress" in No Child Left Behind (NCLB) legislation, with its increasingly punitive consequences, is not much of a motivator—perhaps a little, but only in the very short run.

In "reframing change," Deutschman argues that we must figure out how to motivate people on the basis of their seeing and experiencing that they can feel better (not, in this case, just live longer). The key, then, is how to help people feel and be better.

If feelings and emotions are the key factors, one would think that an appeal to moral purpose in situations of terrible failure would be a great motivator. Again, in most turnaround schools teachers do not feel they are the source of the solution; if anything they are given the message (subtly or not) that they are part of the problem—not much of a motivator there.

Howard Gardner (2004) says that the most important thing to do in changing someone's mind is connect to their reality as the point of departure for change. He warns: "Avoid egocentrism—ensnared in one's own construal of events. The purpose of a mind-changing encounter is not to articulate your own point of view but rather to engage the psyche of the other person" (p. 163).

All change solutions face the too-tight, too-loose dilemma. If a situation is loosely focused, as is the case with schools in need of turnaround, the natural reaction is to tighten things. Command-and-control strategies do get results in these circumstances, but only for a short time and only to a degree. If we then say that we need to give people more leeway—give them resources and trust them to do the right thing—the press for change is lost.

In general terms, the solution to motivating people is to establish the right blend of tightness and looseness, or more accurately to build both into the interactive culture of the organization. I offer some suggestions along these lines shortly, but first it is necessary to loosen our thinking about change, because in situations of turnaround so urgently in need of change, the tendency is to err on the side of tightness. In the United States, the overall legislation of No Child Left Behind and its associated determination of "adequate yearly progress" errs massively on the too-tight side of the problem. The worse the situation, the more laden you are with standards and tests. It is not that this is bad in and of itself; rather, it is grossly distorted in favor of external accountability while being virtually empty of capacity-building strategies that lead to the intrinsic commitment necessary for continuous improvement. Even having the most beautiful standards in the world, you can end up being all dressed up with somewhere to go but with no means of getting there. NCLB does not have the right mixture of motivational means to get better and stay better.

Still, I am in favor of higher standards. We are talking about what is most likely to get us there. Let us open up the question. I have written before about chaos theory, or what we now call complexity theory (Fullan, 2003). Marion (1999, p. xii) explains it this way:

"Chaos theory, or rather that brand of chaos theory that we will identify as complexity theory, responds that order emerges naturally because of unpredictable interaction—interaction is the vehicle by which this occurs and unpredictability is the stimulus that promotes novelty. The argument proposed in this [Marion's] book is that intersecting entities—atoms, molecules, people, organizations—tend (a) to correlate with one another because of their interactions, and (b) to catalyze aggregation [the latter involving new patterns]" (my bracketed insertions).

No politician is going to be elected, or no candidate appointed, to a leadership position on a mission statement base on a platform of unpredictable-interaction, correlation, trust-me-order-will-come. Turnaround schools are already too much like that, and order is not one of the outcomes. But bear with me.

In simple terms, complexity theory says that you cannot force order (the too-tight problem). What if we were to reformulate complexity theory in more practical, understandable terms—have a purpose, increase interaction, increase the flow of quality information, and look for and reinforce promising patterns? This is essentially what the applied-complexity theorists are advocating (still, I say later on that this too is not enough).

Margaret Wheatley (2005), for example, talks about three primary conditions for organizations to make sense of complex circumstances: (1) identity, (2) information, and (3) relationships. Identity involves processes of sense making, or "Who are we and what do we stand for?" Information is the medium of the organization; the flow of quality information with a meaning-making purpose helps to create shared knowledge and, if it goes on long enough, shared wisdom. The third, relationships, are the pathways to intelligence and commitment in the organization ("without connections nothing happens"; Wheatley, 2005, p. 40).

Equally intriguing (but nevertheless insufficient) is Surowiecki's *The Wisdom of Crowds* (2004). Surowiecki makes the case that the "many" are smarter than "the few," and that "chasing the expert" is a costly mistake. He argues that we have to unleash, develop, and cultivate the intellectual and moral commitment of people. He claims there are four conditions for the collective wisdom of crowds to be activated:

1. The members of the organization need to feel *independent* of one another, where people's opinions are not determined by those around them.
2. The members need to be *diverse* enough to represent the range of backgrounds, needs, and interests of the group.
3. They need to be sufficiently *decentralized*, whereby people are able to specialize and draw on local knowledge.
4. There has to be some means, formal or informal, of *aggregation* or turning independent judgment and information into collective decision.

Of course, there are crowds in turnaround schools, and they are not all that wise. Given the seriousness of the problems, we would not want to take the chance of going with independence, diversity, decentralization, and aggregation. But remember, we are engaged at this point in an exercise of loosening our thinking about change and its solutions so that we resist the self-limiting command-and-control strategies (or at least see them as only the first step in a more fundamental series of developments). The wisdom of crowds, for our purposes, is more of an attitude than a concrete plan.

The final idea I would like to explore for liberating our thinking about change is contained in a report with the captivating title "Towards a Million Change Agents" (Bate, Bevan, and Robert; 2005). The authors' focus or concern is the radical reform of the National Health Service System (NHS) in England. Bate and colleagues recognize that regular managerial methods of strengthening performance in a highly complex system are not adequate, and they explore whether the research on "social movements" might permit additional insight into large-scale change. Their review had four objectives:

1. To explore "social movements" as a new way of thinking about large-scale systems change
2. To access the potential contribution of applying this new perspective to NHS improvement
3. To enrich and extend NHS thinking in relation to large-scale, systemwide change
4. To begin to establish a base of research and evidence to support this emergence of an improvement movement in the NHS (p. 2)

Their review is exploratory, and the results are more stimulating than concrete, but the ideas are clearly germane to our interest in going significantly beyond turnaround leadership solutions. Bate and colleagues identified six groups of factors that were related to whether "people are moved or mobilized into collective action and how such mobilization is spread and sustained" (p. 3). These ideas will be familiar to us (how to orchestrate them in a purposeful strategy is another matter):

1. *Rational.* Individuals are driven by self-interest and make rational assessments of the value or gain to themselves of going with others in a social movement.

2. *Emotional.* Movement involvement is compelled from a "feeling" within rather than being a response to an external stimulus; beliefs are more powerful than any personal calculus of costs or potential gains, and it is also emotional rather than task or instrumental relationships that bind the people in a movement together.

3. *Social and normative.* Underlying historical, institutional, and cultural conditions affect the decision to join, support, and remain in a movement; social networks play a key role in recruiting, mobi-

lizing, and retaining participants, and communities of practice can be cultivated as important mechanisms for mobilization.

4. *Behavioral.* Concrete forms of involvement in internal as well as external activities reinforce and sustain support for a movement; shared cultural practices (rituals, celebrations, and so on) strengthen and reaffirm the underpinning cultural and ideological values of the movement.

5. *Organizational.* Some form of enabling organization is required for a movement to grow; resources (financial, time, and human) are important to mobilization.

6. *Leadership.* Movements require individual leaders and a particular kind of multilevel leadership system or process; "framing" is a key leadership activity for igniting collective action and building commitment and consensus for the movement (p. 3).

These ideas are consistent with where we are heading, but mainly serve as insight into which components need to be worked on. The limitations of social movements are that (1) they are unpredictable; (2) they cannot be controlled, neither planned in advance nor managed once under way; (3) they may or may not be good for society; and (4) they are voluntary or semivoluntary such that not everyone who needs to join for large-scale success does join.

In sum, ideas from social movements have potential but must be considered carefully. Oakes and Lipton (2002) strongly criticize the basic change literature for failing to take into account the role of those in power who wish to preserve the status quo for selfish benefit. They discuss the case of Woodrow Wilson High School in the United States, which had a lot of the "right" strategies drawn from the change knowledge base (long-term professional development, lots of communication and dialogue to foster commitment, incremental change, and so on). But in this multiracial, multicultural community, middle-class white parents built their own network (basically a social movement strategy that mobilizes people in a common understanding to engage in action to serve their own ends) to thwart the reformers' educational goals, which were designed to raise the bar and close the gap for African American and Latino students. There are "bad" social movements, so to speak.

Oakes and Lipton call for reformers to combine existing change knowledge and social movement ideas to achieve desired ends. They are short on strategies for how to do so, but this direction is entirely compatible with our analysis in Chapters One and Two. Hargreaves (2003) has gone even further in making compatible suggestions for combining social movement and school improvement strategies, urging educators to (1) rekindle their moral purpose, (2) open their actions and minds to parents and communities concerning their mission, (3) working with unions to become agents of change, and (4) extend professional responsibility beyond their own classrooms to schoolwide and districtwide efforts that improve the system as a whole. But again, how to do this is another matter.

In the too-tight, too-loose world that I am advocating, we would see neither top-down prescription nor site-based management of individual autonomous schools, but rather clusters or networks of schools working together in community and business partnerships to unite the strongest possible motivational forces for reform. It will require sophisticated strategies to get the too-tight/too loose dynamic right—strategies that mobilize local energies, focus on local needs but do so within a state framework of priorities. Local autonomy is not the answer, capacity building with a focus on results is.

In *Turnaround Leadership*, I start with the school side of the equation, suggesting an external commitment to form partnerships with those outside the school. In our experience, the more you build the collective capacity of teachers with good school leadership, the more they see parents and communities as part of the solution instead of the problem. The less the capacity of teachers, the more they attempt to play it safe behind the classroom door or school walls. Confidence and competence breed risk taking of the kind that will bring us new breakthroughs.

I pursue my initial version of these ideas in the next section of this chapter and in Chapter Four. In the meantime, we can draw certain conclusions.

First, the existing approach to turning around schools does not work even in the narrow sense, let alone within the more fundamental goal of sustained improvement in order to reduce the learning gap. There is some hope that politicians and policymakers will be attracted to the ideas in this book because they know in their hearts and minds that current strategies are not getting anywhere on what is the most important social problem of humankind, namely, educating all of its citizens in a healthy and productive society. Bate, Bevan, and Robert (2005) quote Berwick (2003): "At present, prevailing strategies rely largely on outmoded theories of control and standardization of work. More modern and much more effective theories of production seek to harness the imagination and participation of the workforce in reinventing the system" (p. 448). So the first point is to face up to the fact that existing strategies are woefully inadequate, and we know why. This opens the door to more promising—daunting, but exciting—avenues of development.

Second, there are encouraging lines of thinking and development, and we will try to sort some of them out. The mysteries of change stir the pot in the right way, but they do not yield clear answers. We cannot take the chance and go all the way with complexity theory or social movement theory. We can, however, use these and other ideas to strike a balance that addresses the too-tight, too-loose dilemma, crafting a strategy to blend pressure and support in a way that effectively motivates people to lend their ideas and energy to collectively address what needs to be done.

Third, we have put this work in the perspective of the real reform agenda, which is raising the bar and closing the gap in educational performance as part and parcel of reducing the income gap in society—the latter associated with so many powerful social consequences for all of us.

In short, present strategies can move some circumstances from awful to adequate, and in the odd case from adequate to good (albeit not necessarily sustainable). But to move from adequate to good with a continuous press for sustainable, great performance indeed requires "a million change agents" at work. This book is, when all is said and done, about what strategies are most likely to produce and sustain millions of change agents.

The Elements of Successful Change

Drawing on insights from Chapters Two and Three up to this point, we can construct a more sophisticated set of practical strategies that mobilize the forces of change—strategies that do not choose between tightness and looseness but incorporate both. In my view, there are ten key elements for addressing turnaround situations in a way that promises continued success and at the same time makes turnaround part and parcel of the bigger goal of changing the whole system:

1. Define closing the gap as the overarching goal.
2. Attend initially to the three basics.
3. Be driven by tapping into people's dignity and sense of respect.
4. Ensure that the best people are working on the problem.
5. Recognize that all successful strategies are socially based and action oriented—change by doing rather than change by elaborate planning.
6. Assume that lack of capacity is the initial problem and then work on it continuously.
7. Stay the course through continuity of good direction by leveraging leadership.
8. Build internal accountability linked to external accountability.

9. Establish conditions for the evolution of positive pressure.

10. Use the previous nine strategies to build public confidence.

A reminder before proceeding: my colleagues Hargreaves and Fink (2006) say that lists of this kind are a meal, not a menu. You need them all, not any six or seven, because (to stick with the meal metaphor) they feed on each other.

Define Closing the Gap as the Overarching Goal

Raising the bar and closing the gap, as we have seen, is not just a slogan. It captures a host of issues that go to the very core of how a society functions. The first thing is to realize that decreasing the gap between high and low performers—boys, girls, ethnic groups, poor, rich, special education—is crucial because it has so many social consequences. The remaining nine strategic focuses are all in the service of gap closing. I have made it clear in Chapter One that societies must also have economic and social policies focusing on reduction of poverty, and that we must view closing the education gap in that relationship.

The education component can and must be quite precise work; it needs to focus on all categories of students and schools. For example (as I take up in Chapter Four), of the 4,000 elementary schools in Ontario, 497 are classified as having 25 percent or more students from low-income homes; this categorization is called low income cutoff point (LICO) and is based on Statistics Canada data. At the other end of the scale, there are 1,552 schools with 0–5 percent LICO. The province has a current target of reaching 75 percent achievement in reading, writing, and mathematics for sixth grade students. The questions one would want to delve into:

- Of the 497 schools in the low-income category, how many are achieving 75 percent (beating the odds)? What are they doing to be so successful? What can the other schools learn from them?

- Of the 1,552 schools in the high-income category, which schools are not achieving 75 percent (squandering the odds)? What can be done to push them upward? Remember, we are talking about raising the bar for all, not just closing the gap.

- What is the performance gap between the low-income group and the high-income group, and other subgroups therein? Is it being reduced over time?

In our beyond-turnaround world, we need to remind ourselves every day that a sizeable gap is a massive demotivator, for all the reasons we identified in Chapter One. It is not just a matter of being aware of the gap goal, but working on it diligently day after day, monitoring progress, and taking corrective action.

Attend Initially to the Three Basics

You need to work on numerous parts of the problem at once, but the one set of things you should absolutely specialize in is getting the three basics right by age twelve. The three basics are literacy, numeracy, and well-being of students (sometimes called emotional intelligence, character education, safe schools). These are the three legs of the improvement stool.

Well-being serves double duty. It directly supports literacy and numeracy; that is, emotional health is strongly associated with cognitive achievement. It is also indirectly but powerfully part of the educational and societal goal of dealing with the emotional and social consequences of failing and being of low social status. In this sense, political leaders must have an explicit societal agenda of well-being, of which education is one powerful component.

Literacy is not just about reading the words on the page; it includes comprehension, and the skill and joy of being a literate person in a knowledge society. Being numerate is about reasoning and problem solving as much as being good with numbers and figures. The knowledge base is such today (and is growing steadily) that there is no excuse in developed countries for not reaching 90 percent-plus proficiency. My colleagues Peter Hill and Carmel Crévola and I have written a book on how to do this, and many of us are working practically on this in entire provinces or states (see Fullan, Hill, and Crévola, 2006; and the York and Ontario cases in Chapter Four of this book).

The third basic, well-being, is one we all know about but do little to invest in, even though it unlocks just about everything else. A good, concrete example of what I am talking about is the Roots of Empathy program, based in Toronto but spreading across the world (Gordon, 2005). Roots of Empathy brings a mother and her baby together with students in a classroom setting in order to teach children empathy. It is a structured program that has six strands (neuroscience, temperament, attachment, emotional literacy, communication, and social inclusion). A baby and its mother come into a class three times a month from September to June (a class led by a Roots of Empathy instructor and the regular classroom teacher). In the course of one year, bullying and aggression decrease in the school, empathy and inclusion of other students increase, and literacy (reading and writing) increase—because the program works directly on discussion and writing assignments, and because indirect emotional development increases the motivation and engagement necessary for cognitive development.

Two independent external evaluations have found that Roots of Empathy helps children develop the ability to (1) identify others' emotions, (2) understand and explain others' emotions, and (3) be emotionally responsive to others. One external evaluation concluded that "Roots of Empathy program children, relative to comparison children, exhibited significant increases in emotional understanding and pro-social behaviors and significant decreases in aggressive behaviors [in fact, comparison children exhibited significant *increases* in aggression over the school year]" (Gordon, 2005, p. 247).

Furthermore, "When changes were examined in only those children demonstrating some form of aggression at pre-test . . . it was found that 67 percent of Roots of Empathy program children *de-creased* [aggression] at post-test, whereas 64 percent of comparison children *increased*" (p. 248, *emphasis* in original).

The focus on well-being requires more than Roots of Empathy, but my point is to elevate emotional safety and development as a crucial foundational goal meshed with cognitive achievement. Clearly with respect to the third basic, well-being, there are a host of nonschooling policies that must be pursued, ranging from early child care to improvements in housing, health care, parenting, neighborhoods, and jobs.

In a much more fundamental and integrated way, England has tackled the well-being of children through its Every Child Matters (2003) agenda. After wide consultation with the public, educators, and yes, children themselves, England formed their new policy around five basic goals for children: (1) being healthy, (2) staying safe, (3) enjoying and achieving, (4) making a positive contribution, and (5) economic well-being. More than rhetoric, England replaced local education authorities (school districts) with local authorities within which schools, health, and related social agencies are integrated in single services. Directors (superintendents) of education were replaced with new CEOs, titled directors of children's services. This is a radical and bold move to take well-being the full distance.

Within schools, my emphasis on the three basics—literacy, numeracy, and well-being—is not to say, "Do not work on other goals." But the three basics are a priority and can operate as a set. If you can get them right, a lot of other things will fall into place. In effect, the three basics are the essential foundations for living in the knowledge economy of the twenty-first century.

Be Driven by Tapping into People's Dignity and Respect

Some students and teachers do not deserve respect, but the reason I emphasize this goal is that it is the key to people's feelings and thus to their motivation. Again, the set of ten is a meal and not a menu; the ten strategies in concert will help turn disrespect around. Teachers in turnaround schools feel (and are made to feel) unworthy, and whether this is deserved is not the motivational point.

To take an extreme example, the research literature on violence clearly shows that the trigger to violent acts is people feeling they are disrespected and threatened with loss of face. We saw this theme with Wilkinson (2005) in Chapter One. Wilkinson quotes Gilligan: "I have yet to see a serious act of violence that was not provoked by the experience of feeling shamed and humiliated, disrespected and ridiculed, and that did not represent the attempt to prevent or undo this 'loss of face'—no matter how severe the punishment, even if it includes death" (Gilligan, 1996, p. 110).

As Gilligan says, "disrespect" is so central to modern psychodynamics that it has been abbreviated into the slang term "he dissed me." Violence is at the extreme end of the dissing spectrum, but there can be no doubt that teachers in publicly named failing schools feel dissed; and it is not a motivator to do good things. As an aside, just as we saw in Chapter One that dissed people often engage in "downward discrimination" in which they mistreat those who are next in line in the status hierarchy—a kind of kick-the-cat syndrome—it may be that some teachers in turnaround schools, because they are constantly devalued, become unconsciously less caring of their students.

The goal in getting out of this vicious cycle is to suspend pejorative judgment at the initial stages of working with turnaround schools. (In fact, one could make the case that in schools that are well off in terms of resources and community, teachers who do not serve their students well deserve to be dissed more than those in challenging schools that are not doing well.)

An interesting and much-neglected take on respect in the teaching profession is Elizabeth Campbell's original contribution (2003, 2005) in uncovering issues related to unethical behavior among teachers. Campbell interviewed teachers about their relationship with colleagues concerning ethical matters regarding treatment of students. With remarkable directness, she states that the purpose of her study was "to explore the ubiquitous norms of collegial loy-alty, noninterference, and solidarity that foster school climates in which students' best interests are not necessarily supported" (Camp-bell, 2005, p. 207). Ironically, she observes, despite all the talk of professional learning communities one of the most entrenched norms of collegiality "is one which equates ethical treatment of col-leagues with a kind of unquestioned loyalty, group solidarity, and an essential belief that teachers as professionals should not interfere in the business of other teachers, criticize them or their practices, or expose their possibly negligent or harmful behavior, even at the expense of students' well-being" (p. 209).

Campbell provides numerous examples of teachers witnessing unethical behavior on the part of colleagues but not doing anything about it. She talks about Roger, a middle school teacher who saw a colleague physically hurt a student intentionally and then lie about it afterward. Roger's fear of confronting a colleague inhibited him from addressing the matter. Campbell says that many teachers in her sample come to "accept that the best way to keep out of trou-ble in schools is to avoid challenging colleagues on matters of com-petence and ethical conduct and learn to live with the guilt over their inaction" (p. 214). Campbell also discusses the student teacher who recalled how her supervising teacher walked by a grade five stu-dent who had rather large ears that protruded; the teacher flicked the student's ear with a snapping motion that made it turn pink. The student was quietly sitting at his desk, and all the teacher said was "I couldn't resist" as the rest of the class laughed in response. These norms of collegial loyalty serve "to close down collective and reflective dialogue rather than embrace it" (p. 215).

My argument here is subtle, so I will be explicit. This is about dignity and respect as a source of motivation. Clearly, students who are not respected are not motivated to learn. Jean Rudduck and her colleagues (1996) have consistently found that students are more or less motivated according to whether they are treated with re-spect. Note that I am also saying the same thing applies to teachers in failing schools in terms of how they are treated by the outside. It is only speculation on my part, but all the sociopsychological dynamics of failing schools tell me that Campbell would find more examples of unethical behavior on the part of teachers in failing schools than in well-off schools. I am not talking about all or even most teachers, but downtrodden teachers are more likely to engage, unwittingly or otherwise, in downward discrimination.

This chapter is still about motivation, so the solution is not to go around fingering badly behaved teachers (although in extreme cases that would be necessary). Like Campbell, I favor a socially based solution. The set of recommendations I am suggesting in this chapter serves to improve the conditions for improvement. In other words, through better conditions the strategies show in effect greater respect for the teachers working in these circumstances. I am also saying with Campbell that fostering professional learning communities should include forums for teachers to collectively reflect on and collaborate on the ethical and moral dimensions of their work and behavior. Because these are collective forums not tied to the latest specific incident, they need not be threatening. Ethical behavior clearly fits with my emphasis on the moral imperative (Fullan, 2003). In fact, one of the three components of moral purpose that I identified is how we treat each other, by showing "demanding respect," that is, mutual caring and mutual expectations to contribute to the betterment of the school (Fullan, 2005). The other two aspects are a commitment to raise the bar and close the gap, and to improve the social environment by contributing to development of other schools.

Professional learning communities should not be confined to the latest ideas and innovations. And they should not be places for well-meaning but superficial exchanges. Especially in schools, where emotions run high, these communities must foster an open exchange where teachers can explore elements of their own practice that they see as ethically responsive or problematic. The goal is to simultaneously empathize with teachers in difficult circumstances while calling for and reinforcing higher ethical standards. Schools that promote trust in this way are more likely to motivate people all around, and in turn more likely to do better (that is, more likely to turn around). Bryk and Schneider's findings (2002) in *Trust in Schools* are similar. Interestingly, they found that the higher the trust in the school the more likely that action would be taken in relation to teachers who were mistreating students.

Thus it is not that you never disrespect a given teacher; rather, it is not a good motivational starting point. In extreme cases, formal disciplinary action is required. But for most teachers' daily motivation, good solid social support is essential. The ten strategic elements being used in concert help sort out those who truly deserve the label of disrespect (see especially the one on positive pressure). The vast majority of teachers in the course of a good, sustained turnaround process will respond to solutions in which they see students motivated and engaged for the first time and when they are working with colleagues and teachers who support them and have good ideas.

It is obvious that dignity and respect are crucial for relating to downtrodden parents and neighborhoods. It is beyond the scope of this book to take up community-based strategies, but as I said earlier, as schools develop capacities using the elements described here they extend their involvement with the outside. The school of the future is not autonomous; it will have many forms of engagement with the outside as part and parcel of improving the system as a whole.

Ensure That the Best People Are Working on the Problem

We saw earlier from Minthrop (2004) and Kanter (2004) that when things go wrong and there is little constructive help from the outside, the more talented leave the scene. They have more options, and it is depressing to work in a failing school that has little chance of becoming good. We also saw that some of the most talented never show up in the first place because policies and practices work against the flow of teachers most appropriate for schools in difficulty (Levin, Mulhern, and Schunck, 2005).

The opposite must happen. The more talented are needed precisely because the challenges are greater. Governments and districts can foster incentives and other resources for principals and teachers to work in challenging circumstances. If the right combination of strategies and support is marshaled, turnaround situations can become successful, and this can be where the best educators get their satisfaction. In England, for example, the government has just asked its National College of School Leadership to develop a proposal and program based on identifying effective school principals who would form a cadre of National School Leaders (NLE), to be given incentives and support to work in the most challenging circumstances. This approach must also furnish incentives for attracting the best teachers in numbers to work with school leaders. The idea is to make it prestigious in the profession to help improve the most difficult situations—getting the best people to work on the problem. I am not advocating this particular solution, but the concept of getting the more talented principals and teachers on the scene rather than the less talented (the situation in many turnaround schools) is critical. In other words, reverse the current incentive system.

It is obvious that leadership is crucial in all of this. Kanter (2004) captures this well when she says, "The fundamental task of leaders is to develop confidence in advance of victory, in order to attract the investments that make victory possible—money, talent, support, empathy, attention, effort, or people's best thinking" (p. 19).

Once you start gaining on the close-the-gap problem, there will be fewer cases of extreme challenge. In countries where the gap is not as great as in others, they already have more favorable circumstances. In Ontario, for example, there are only 509 (of 4,000) elementary schools with highly challenging circumstances as measured by percentage (25 plus) of students living in poverty, and some of these schools are already performing well. What if there were a concerted effort to get some of the best educators along with strong policy and resource support to tackle the situation? What is needed is to turn around momentum in a way that creates a new, continuous winning streak.

I need to make a more fundamental point here. By using the strategies I am suggesting, the overall talent in the system increases. The talent in the system improves as people's potential is unlocked; some may leave, and others are attracted to the profession. Motivated people get better at their work.

Recognize That All Successful Strategies Are Socially Based and Action Oriented

This element takes us back to Wilkinson (2005). He found that the most important determinants of health (and, I should say, motivation to do good things) include "the nature of early childhood experience, the amount of anxiety and worry we suffer, the quality of our social relationship, the amount of control we have over our lives, and our social status" (p. 9). All but early childhood are wrapped up in turnaround school situations: anxiety is high, relationships are poor, control is low, and social status is at the bottom. A core strategy, then, must be to improve relationships, because doing so addresses this set of problems. All successful turnarounds develop collaboration where there was none before. When relationships develop, trust increases, as do other measures of social capital and social cohesion.

This represents a difficult challenge, but again the set of ten elements working together makes it possible. The fact that all successful strategies are socially based is reinforced all the time when we develop professional learning communities (PLCs) that were not there before (DuFour, Eaker, and DuFour, 2005). This is why Kanter identifies collaboration as one of three key elements in confidence and winning streaks (the other two are accountability and initiative, both of which are reinforced by collaboration). Restoring people's confidence, says Kanter, refines four kinds of action:

1. Getting connected in new ways through conversation

2. Carrying out important work jointly

3. Communicating respect

4. Demonstrating inclusion (that everyone is part of the picture; p. 241)

This is why Deutschman, in his "Change or Die" article (2005), found that the only situation under which heart patients improved was when the change process was "buttressed with weekly support groups" (p. 4).

Socially based strategies can help with another huge problem (and opportunity for improvement), one that all researchers on school improvement know about but few act on with any intensity. I speak here of the well-known research finding that variations in student achievement are greater across classrooms within a school than across schools. Once you factor out the role of input qualities (that is, once you start to measure the value added by the school) the biggest factor at work is the individual teachers, and they differ from classroom to classroom within a school.

In a carefully controlled experiment in which teachers were randomly assigned classrooms, Nye, Konstantopoulos, and Hedges (2004) found that "the difference among teachers [within a school] is substantial in comparison to the variance between schools. In reading, the between-teacher variance component is over twice as large as [the] between-school variance component at grade two and over three times as large at grade three. . . . This suggests that naturally occurring teacher effects are larger than naturally occurring school effects" (p. 247). I return shortly to the phrase "naturally occurring."

Put more starkly, the difference for a student's learning and achievement between getting an effective or an ineffective teacher is huge. Of special interest to us, the range of effectiveness in low-SES schools is greater. In both high-SES and low-SES schools, between-teacher variance is greater than between-school, but in low-SES schools *the pattern is more pronounced*. As Nye and colleagues put it, "In low SES schools, it matters more *which* teacher a child receives than it does in high SES schools" (p. 254, italics in original).

Where does this lead? Let's merge three things: (1) class-to-class variations in teacher effectiveness within schools are large and most consequential; (2) these variations exist in naturally occurring ways, that is, they persist if you do nothing explicitly to alter them; and (3) all effective change strategies are socially based. We must as a consequence focus on reducing bad variation within schools (and, I say later, on bad variation across like schools—apple to apple comparisons). Thus the more you develop active professional learning communities within schools in which teachers observe each other's teaching, and work with school leadership to make ongoing improvements, the greater the consistency and quality of teaching across the whole school, at which point all students in the school benefit and keep on benefiting. The more you de-privatize teaching in a purposeful way, the more you improve teaching, learning, and student achievement. This is easier said than done.

To start with intraschool variance, the goal has to be to find what motivates teachers to work on this problem. We are finding that this is going to be a lot harder than it sounds. One puzzle is to ask why so many teachers everywhere are disgruntled despite a high level of intrinsic commitment to their work. We need, in other words, to change working conditions that get at and leverage intrinsic motivation, that open classroom doors, initially within the school, in order to develop quality with greater consistency across classrooms within schools. At first glance, strategies based on developing professional learning communities look like the answer, and I do support their directional value. But a lot of the evidence indicates that PLCs (or any other strategy) are not making their way with any substance and continuity inside the classroom. It may happen here and there, but not on any scale we need if we are to close the gap. We saw from Campbell (2005) how supremely difficult it is to change teacher norms of autonomy and loyalty. The Cross City Campaign for Urban School Reform (2005) study we referred to in

Chapter One, despite millions and millions of dollars and a lot of the right strategies, in the final analysis could not penetrate the classroom door.

Richard Elmore (2004a, 2004b) has been telling us for years that current strategies are not getting at the core of improving instructional practice in the classroom. Elmore laments: "Educators equate professionalism with autonomy—getting to use their own judgment, to exercise discretion, to determine the conditions of their own work in classrooms and schools. In fact, professionalism outside of education is exactly the opposite of this definition. Professionals gain their social authority not by exercising autonomy, but by subscribing to an externally-validated body of knowledge, by agreeing to have their discretion limited by that knowledge, and by facing sanctions if they operate outside that body of knowledge" (2004a, p. 3).

If the threat of death does not motivate people who are ill, what on earth is going to motivate teachers to change? The answer has to be deep engagement with other colleagues and with mentors in exploring, refining, and improving their practice as well as setting up an environment in which this not only can happen but is encouraged, rewarded, and pressed to happen. This begs part of the question of how to do so, but let us finally admit that there is no other way. My conclusion is similar to Elmore's as he comments on some of the work he is doing with practitioners, helping them to get inside instructional practice: "The theory of action behind [this process of examining practice] might be stated as follows: The development of systematic knowledge about, and related to, large–scale instructional improvement requires a change in the prevailing culture of administration and teaching in schools. Cultures do not change by mandate; they change by the specific displacement of existing norms, structures, and processes by others; the process of cultural change depends fundamentally on modeling the new values and behavior that you expect to displace the existing ones" (2004a, p. 11).

The only way we can accomplish the changes we need is through intense focus on improving classroom practice. We can do it by declaring that this is the focus: reduce bad variation by increasing consistency. Teachers and teacher leaders will have to take some risks here. It is one area that is both powerful and within the control of teachers: break down the autonomy of the classroom so that greater consistency of effective practice can be achieved. Really, compared to the status quo there is little risk. In this more focused and intense work, teachers learn every day. They learn in context. There is nothing that better motivates people to make more investments of time, energy, and commitment than to grow better at something that has importance. Failure may be the initial motivator, but it is increased competence that leads us to do more and more.

We have suggested in our *Breakthrough* book a plan for systematically involving all schools and school systems in improving elementary school reform. It requires a full press toward intensive and focused improvement of all classrooms and schools in a given system. We think that this is achievable within our lifetime (Fullan, Hill, and Crévola, 2006).

My initial focus was on within-school variation across classes, but the big solution is not just about intraschool improvement. We have found that collaboration across schools and districts—what we call lateral capacity building—pays enormous dividends in relation to new knowledge and wider commitments (Fullan, 2005). This network or cluster-based strategy can do double duty. The impact of school cluster networks can be used to reduce both intraschool classroom-to-classroom variations as well as school-to-school differences. We need to pounce on reducing the two.

Socially based strategies, such as collaboration and support, when combined with the other nine elements become demandingly interactive. There is no stronger accountability than when it is reinforced daily with peers working on important problems in which internal and external transparency is evident.

Several of our guidelines reinforce the notion that purposeful action is the route to new breakthroughs. Socially based strategies mean that the emphasis is on doing rather than elaborate planning.

This point is brought home powerfully in Doug Reeves's study (2006). Reeves found that the size of the planning document is inversely related to the amount and quality of implementation! In a large sample involving 280,000 students and three hundred schools, schools were scored on seventeen separate indicators related to adherence to the state or district's formal requirements of the school improvement plans. The scores were then related to student achievement results: "The stunning finding is that the 'prettiness' of the plan is inversely (or should we say perversely?) related to student achievement" (p. 64). Of those schools having high conformity with planning requirements, 25.6 percent of students scored proficient or higher on assessments compared to 46.3 percent achievement for schools with low conformity to planning requirements.

This is not a message that says abandon all planning. It means reduce the distance between planning and action—formal planning documents are less important than (indeed interfere with) implementation, execution, and monitoring. Put another way, the planning is built into the doing, feedback, and corrective action.

Reeves's finding was brought home in our own recent work in Ontario (see Chapter Four), where we are implementing a province-wide strategy to improve literacy and numeracy for all seventy-two districts and four thousand elementary schools. We recently conducted case studies of eight districts that seemed to have sound strategies (along the lines of this book) and were getting results as measured by three-year trends in student achievement (Campbell and Fullan, 2006). One of the cases is a francophone board just outside Ottawa: Conseil des écoles catholiques de langue française du centre-est (CECLFCE).

Prior to initiating our new capacity-building strategy, CECLFCE engaged in the practice of requiring school improvement plans, which listed all activities that were to be held throughout the year, resulting in documents (Reeves calls this the disease of "documentarianism") fifty pages thick or more. In the new era, the district emphasized a few key standards tied to action that would address student achievement. The written plans are now brief, less formal, and geared to action, monitoring, rapid feedback, and focused instructional improvement, including teachers learning from each other as well as schools and the district working interactively. After years of bureaucratic requirements and stagnated student achievement scores, the CECLFCE is now on the move, with increased student achievement in each of the last three years and with more to come.

Assume That Lack of Capacity Is the Initial Problem and Then Work on It Continuously

Another guideline that is action based and powerful is capacity building. In a sense, all ten elements address capacity building, which I defined earlier as a policy, strategy, or action taken that increases the collective efficacy of a group to improve student learning through new knowledge, enhanced resources, and greater motivation on the part of people working individually and together.

The emphasis here is to rein in judgment at the early part of a turnaround process in favor of working on capacity building. Assume, in other words, that one reason the situation is not working is that people do not know how to improve it, or they do not believe it can be improved. At this stage, judgment is not a good motivator and is not perceived as fair (at later stages judgment can be ramped up, so to speak, once it can be positioned as fair). The reason we want to spark the motivation of all people or the majority is this is what it will take for sustainable success—the wisdom and commitment of the crowd.

This emphasis on capacity building at the early stages is consistent with our knowledge about how people change. To secure new beliefs and higher expectations—critical to a turnaround situation—people first need new experiences that lead them to different beliefs. The review of research on social movements by Bate and colleagues led them to conclude that "radical change often involves a collective, interactional, and emergent process of learning and sense making" (Bate, Bevan, and Robert, 2005, p. 24). More explicitly they concluded: "Just as early studies in employee participation showed, workers did not have a high propensity to participate prior to the experience of participation; this came after, not before the experience. Put idiomatically, people cannot want 'it' until they have tried it. . . . The concrete experience of participating in a movement is crucial, meanings and value being formed *after the experience* not before it" (p. 31, my italics). This is another reason action is more important than developing elaborate planning documents.

All of this is consistent with Reeves (2006), our own work on change (behaviors change before beliefs), and Pfeffer and Sutton's findings (2000) on the barriers to closing the knowing-doing gap. They found five big barriers to action:

1. When talk or planning substitutes for action

2. When memory is a substitute for thinking (we have always done it this way)

3. When fear prevents acting on knowledge (big problem for turnaround cases)

4. When measurement obstructs good judgment

5. When internal competition turns friends into enemies (a lot of initial blame goes on in failing schools)

Essentially Pfeffer and Sutton conclude, as I do, that you need an early start in acting on the solution. They put it this way: "Embed more of the process of acquiring new knowledge in the actual doing of the task and less in formal training programs that are frequently ineffective" (p. 27). Capacity building first, and judgment second—because this is what will motivate more people. Learning in context and learning every day are the keys. Capacity-building experiences develop skills, clarity (as you become more skilled, you become more specifically clear), and motivation. Since these are generated collectively—that is, shared by the group—they become potent new forces for breakthrough improvement.

Another reason capacity-building strategies work is they give people concrete experiences that improvement is possible. People need proof that there is some reality to the higher expectations. Kanter (2004) says that pep talks or inspiring speeches are not convincing, or at least not for long: "That's why winning [new experiences that work]—or its closer approximation—is often necessary before people believe they can win" (p. 40). Positive experience is what is motivating.

Stay the Course Through Continuity of Good Direction; Leverage Leadership

In situations of awful performance, tightening the focus through greater control (but again, being low on judgment) is necessary at the beginning of the turnaround process. What we saw earlier, however, is that there is little continuity to build on initial partial success in order to go deeper (in turn to obtain the commitment and wisdom of the crowd). Staying the course means that careful attention is paid to developing leadership of others in the organization in the interests of continuity and deepening of good direction.

Leaders developing other leaders is at the heart of sustainability. It is Hargreaves and Fink's third principle, that "sustainable leadership spreads. It sustains as well as depends on the leadership of others" (2006, p. 95). It is the last of my own eight principles of sustainability: "the long lever of leadership" (Fullan, 2005, p. 27). It is why I have concluded, for example, that the main mark of a principal at the end of his or her tenure is not just the impact on the bottom line of student achievement but equally how many good leaders the principal leaves behind who can go even further. You have to be around for a while to accomplish that, and the system must develop leadership-succession policies with this goal in mind.

Staying the course is crucial because initial gains in a turnaround situation are fragile and unclear. Kanter goes so far as to call it

"Kanter's Law": "Everything can look like a failure in the middle" (p. 67). Wins, she says, are a result of persistence, of not giving up when everything seems to be in jeopardy (pp. 67–68).

In turnaround situations, we need to stay the course because it takes a while to change the experiences and behavior of people and "to shift the emotional and investment climate" that is at the core of new motivations (Kanter, 2004, p. 292).

Build Internal Accountability Linked to External Accountability

Richard Elmore (2004b) helped us define internal accountability earlier. It is when individual responsibility, collective expectations, and accountability data within the school are aligned. The exact same data look very different if the organization has the capacity for internal accountability. Data can be empowering or disabling; details, metrics, measurement, analyses, charts, tests, assessments, performance evaluations, report cards, and grades are the tools of accountability, but they are not neutral tools. They do not restore confidence by themselves. What matters is the culture that surrounds them. For losers, this is another sign that they are watched too closely, not trusted, and about to be punished. For winners, they are useful, even vital, tools for understanding and improving performance. People embrace tools of accountability when they are in control and when the information empowers them and helps them succeed (Kanter, 2004).

External accountability does not work unless it is accompanied by development of internal accountability. This is why assessment for learning is such a powerful, high-yield strategy. It helps people clarify goals and where they are in relation to achieving them, and it gives them a tool for improvement by linking performance data with changes in instruction needed to increase achievement.

Turnaround schools have to be helped in the transition from being confronted with the brutal facts to using data to get at improvement, and eventually for celebrating progress. If the other capacities in our set of ten are cultivated, sooner rather than later people not only become more comfortable with data but seek data. It is at this point that external accountability becomes more accepted, more transparently available, and more readily used for summative conclusions and judgments.

Establish Conditions for Evolution of Positive Pressure

Positive pressure is pressure that motivates. It is pressure that works both ways—government to schools and vice versa—and it is pressure that is seen as fair and reasonable. If some schools are performing poorly while facing highly challenging circumstances, governments have the responsibility of (and should be held accountable for) investing in greater capacity building. If schools receive more resources, they should feel the pressure to improve. Collaborative cultures lend support but also contain powerful peer pressures.

The evolution of positive pressure means taking all the excuses off the table. As we add resources, new capacities, and examples of other (similar) schools that are being more successful, reducing the distractors (unnecessary paper work, ineffective bureaucratic procedures, bad industrial relations with unions, and so on), eventually being judgmental relative to a situation of persistent bad or mediocre performance is justified.

The idea is to evolve a system where there is left no legitimate reason to be unsuccessful. Put another way, once you strip away all the possible legitimate excuses it should be seen as fair and reasonable by most people to ask whether it is the quality of leadership and the quality of teaching that is to blame in a given problematic situation. Once you establish conditions where the vast majority of people are motivated to improve things, the problems worth being judgmental about are more obvious.

Build Public Confidence

You know that you are successful when public confidence soars. Confidence is not granted by requesting it in advance of performance. It is a chicken-and-egg problem: we need support to perform better, and better performance garners further support. The social contract with society is, on the one hand, for education to do its utmost to reduce the gap of performance across its schools and subgroups as part of creating a more equal society, for all the reasons we discussed in Chapter One; and on the other hand for society to invest more in education, tentatively and provisionally at first but willingly once progress is evident and continuous. Some of the public confidence I have in mind is local, a direct result of partnering with the community. Other endorsements are more societal, as when people generally value the public school system for its role in closing the educational gap as a crucial part of improving economic and health conditions for all.

Kanter (2004) calls external confidence "a network to provide resources": "Winning makes it easier to attract financial backers, loyal customers, enthusiastic fans, talented recruits, media attention, opinion leader support, and political goodwill. Continuing to win stimulates the network to grow in size, scope, and magnitude of investment" (p. 30). Or later: "The ultimate work of leaders lies in the connection between their groups and the wider network that provides support, loyalty, revenues, or capital. Leaders must prove to those in the wider circle that their investments are warranted" (p. 341).

Even more directly for us: "Public school leaders had to build credibility with elected officials, school boards, parents, neighborhood groups, and the press by showing that stakeholders' goals and needs would help shape plans for turning around low-performing schools" (p. 342).

To accomplish this, leaders must use the ten elements of successful change discussed in this section to motivate and obtain the individual and collective involvement of everyone in the organization necessary to pull this off.

What this accomplishes is to create the conditions under which the vast majority of teachers will be motivated to invest in success. Such motivation is contagious because you get more support and pressure, both technically (knowledge) and emotionally. My colleague Ken Leithwood (2005) recently completed an excellent synthesis of research evidence on the theme of teacher working conditions that matter. The eight factors he identified that affect teachers' motivation and performance are entirely compatible with our discussion:

1. Individual sense of professional efficiency
2. Collective sense of professional efficacy
3. Organizational commitment
4. Job satisfaction
5. Stress and burnout
6. Morale
7. Engagement or disengagement from the school and the profession
8. Pedagogical content knowledge (p. 2)

The relationship between Leithwood's list and my ten elements is that he is reporting on research findings, while I am proposing strategies to *produce* the positive end of each of his factors. In addition, following Wilkinson, I have said that teachers feel doubly disaffected if they are working under poor conditions, and they and everyone else know that they are much worse off than their more-privileged colleagues. The relative deprivation of being at the lower end of a wide scale of inequality as measured by the gap between low- and high-performing schools adds emotional insult to injury. (I wonder, as an aside here, whether teachers who teach in failing schools have a shorter life expectancy; Wilkinson's research would tell us that this is likely.) Closing the gap increases positive feelings in its own right, and it makes people feel better relative to the bigger scheme of things.

Raising the bar and closing the gap is a social problem that requires a social solution. The mobilization of many will be required.

The ten elements of successful change increase the probability of this happening by striking the right balance of tightness and looseness to tap into the sources of motivational commitment and energy. In our successful cases we see a deeper shift from "my" to "our":

- In the school, individual teachers stop thinking about "my classroom" and start thinking about "our school."

- In the districts, individual school leaders stop thinking about "my school" and start thinking about "our schools or districts."

- Across districts, individual district leaders stop thinking about "my district" and start thinking about "our districts, state, or province."

- Across states or provinces, state leaders stop thinking about "my state" and start thinking about "our country."

- Dare to go global!

Now we are talking about a social movement. The task at hand does indeed require a million change agents, not a few good leaders. The next question is how to mobilize whole systems to engage in deep, comprehensive, purposeful reform that makes a difference for all students.

4

Turning a Whole System Around

A s I sit here on Christmas Eve 2005, thinking about moral purpose, valuing all that is great about humanity, images of moral
purpose come dancing in my head. It is appropriate, then, to consider the question of turning a whole system around.

My reverie is disturbed as I recall one of the latest online research reports on my computer. The title of the report grabs me: *The
Funding Gap 2005: Low-Income and Minority Students Shortchanged
by Most States* (Education Trust, 2005). The report analyzes educational expenditure by state and finds that states spend on the average $900 *less* per year in the school districts with the poorest
students. Three states spend more: Massachusetts, Minnesota, and
New Jersey, but most (twenty-seven of forty-nine states) spend less,
some as high as $2,280 per pupil (New York) and $2,065 (Illinois).
(Note that these expenditures do not include money from foundations and federal funds, but as the report says these latter funds are
intended to supplement and not substitute for state expenditures;
there are some states and courts that are moving to fix inequitable
distribution of money, but the problem remains critical.)

The Education Trust report then proposes that students in poverty require additional funding, which is commonly accepted as a
40 percent increase. Once this 40 percent adjustment is incorporated, thirty-eight states spend less than they should, with a per student shortfall of $1,436. Even without the 40 percent adjustment,

the difference is huge. In New York, for example in a class of twenty-five students the difference is $57,000; in two elementary schools of four hundred students the difference becomes $912,000, and between two typical high schools of fifteen hundred students a whopping $3,420,000.

Even small differences have serious consequences. Take Colorado, where the gap is only $101 per student. For a classroom of twenty-five students this means $2,525, which could pay for a classroom library of 250 books. For a standard elementary school of four hundred students, the difference of $40,400 would come close to paying for a reading specialist. For a high school, the difference of $151, in a school of five hundred students, could pay for three literacy coaches.

There are also gaps within districts. In many districts (Los Angeles Unified School District, for example) negotiated contracts between unions and districts give teachers the right to transfer to other schools as they gain seniority. The more senior teachers select "better" schools. The end result is less-experienced teachers in high-poverty schools. In one comparison between two Los Angeles schools, the difference in budget was $1 million for teacher salaries.

Money isn't everything, but it makes a difference if targeted in the ways advocated in this book. In Massachusetts, where the money differential has been addressed since 1993, according to the 2005 National Assessment of Educational Progress fourth and eight graders outperformed students in every other state in reading and math. To be specific, in 1992, 23 percent of Massachusetts fourth graders were proficient in math standards; in 2005, 49 percent were proficient.

Need I say that you cannot close the achievement gap by widening the expenditure gap? It gets worse. A statement from the National School Board's association is entitled "Congress Utterly Fails in Its Commitment to America's Schoolchildren" (Schmidt, 2005). It reports on the end-of-session legislation for 2005, which includes a 1 percent cut in funds for public education, along with creation of a private school voucher program that was attached (bootlegged) as part of a hurricane relief program.

I have made the case in earlier chapters that the real reform agenda is to reduce the income gap between the highest and lowest earners in society and that failure to address this problem has enormous, negative individual and social consequences for society. When public education seriously underfunds the poor, it puts the schools in question in a position of perpetuating the problem through their inability to get education to do its share of gap reduction by improving the educational achievement of the disadvantaged. Education reflects society's priorities and then returns on that investment. In this case of low investment it perpetuates the status quo of wide income differentials, indeed worsening the problem.

It is hard enough to achieve reform without additional money, let alone compounding the problem by reducing the basic budget. But money by itself is not the answer. Even major efforts with serious additional dollars (from foundations, for example) have difficulty penetrating classroom practice. The Cross City Campaign for Urban School Reform (2005) reports on case studies from Chicago, Milwaukee, and Seattle. All three systems had the attention of political leaders at all levels of the system, focused on many of the seemingly "right things" such as literacy and math, used obvious choice strategies such as concentration on assessment for learning data, invested heavily in professional development, developed new leadership, and focused on systemwide change.

And they had money—Seattle with $35 million in external funds, Milwaukee with extra resources and flexibility, and Chicago with more money than it had ever seen. There was huge pressure, but success was not expected overnight. Decision makers and the public would have been content to see growing success over a five- or even ten-year period.

The up-front conclusion of the case study evaluators: "The three districts we studied had decentralized resources and authority to the schools in different ways and had undergone significant organizational changes to facilitate their ambitious, instructional improvement plans. The unfortunate reality for the many principals and teachers we interviewed is that the districts were unable to change and improve practice on a large scale" (Cross City Campaign, 2005, p. 4).

The lack of success is discouraging because the strategies employed appeared to incorporate many of the elements recommended by change strategists: "Academic standards and instructional frameworks, assessment and accountability systems, and professional development for standards-based instruction are among the tools of systemic reform that are used to change classroom instruction" (p. 23).

Thus we see "standards-based" systemwide reform that sounds as if it should work. So what is the problem? In my view, the strategy lacks a focus on what needs to change in instructional practice. In Chicago, teachers did focus on standards and coverage, but in interviews they "did not articulate any deep changes in teaching practice that may have been under way" (p. 23). Furthermore, "Instructional goals were more often articulated in terms of student outcomes or achievement levels than in terms of instructional quality, that is, *what the schools do* to help students achieve" (p. 29; italics in original).

Milwaukee reveals similar problems relative to achieving instructional improvements while using greater decentralization in the context of system support and competitive choice. The focus was on literacy; a literacy coach was housed in every school in the district, and considerable professional development and technical support services were available. Education plans for each school were to focus on literacy standards through (1) data analysis and assessment and (2) subject-area achievement targets including literacy across the curriculum.

Sounds like a convincing strategy. However, what is missing again is the black box of instructional practice in the classroom.

The case writers observe: "We placed the Education Plan in the indirect category due to its non-specificity regarding regular or desired instructional content and practices" (p. 49).

More generally, the report concludes that although these serious districtwide reform initiatives "appeared" to prioritize instruction, they did so indirectly (through standards, assessment, leadership responsibilities). However, in the experience of principals and teachers, the net effect was that "policies and signals were non-specific regarding intended effects on classroom teaching and learning" (p. 65).

The third case, Seattle, is a variation on the same theme. The game plan looks good. Standards defined the direction while the district's Transformational Academic Achievement Planning process "was designed as a vehicle for helping schools develop their own strategy for (1) helping all students meet standards, and (2) eliminating the achievement gap between white students and students of color" (p. 66). As in Milwaukee, the district reorganized to support site-based management, including allocation of considerable resources to schools. The case writers observe: "The recent effort to become a standards-based district was one of the first sustained instructional efforts with direct attention to teaching and learning. However, the conversations district leaders had about standards *were rarely connected to changes in instruction*" (p. 69; my italics).

The report continues: "At the school level, finding teachers who understood the implications of standards for their teaching was difficult" (p. 72).

I highlight the three cases of Chicago, Milwaukee, and Seattle to show how difficult education reform is going to be, even if you have a lot going for you. This is why in this book I advocate standing back from the issue, taking the wider and more fundamental perspective on the role of public education in societal improvement, and understanding the psychology of failure so that we can develop strategies with far more power to turn the losing streak of failing schools into a winning streak of continuous improvement.

Turning a System Around

In the last few years, we have turned attention to what I call the trilevel development solution (Barber and Fullan, 2005). This is system reform in action and involves: What has to happen at the school and community level? the district level? the level of the state (admittedly needing to differentiate between state and federal where applicable)? The idea is to "cause" developments, along the lines of this book, within and across the three levels. It is not so much seeking alignment as it is experiencing permeable connectivity—lots of two-way horizontal and vertical mutual influence.

At the state level, we are engaged in five locations (and possibly more in the near future) in four countries: South Australia and New South Wales in Australia, England, Washington State in the United States, and Ontario, Canada. In this chapter I use our work in one district in Ontario (and Ontario as a full system) to illustrate *beyond*-turnaround leadership in practice.

York Region District School Board (YRDSB)

York Region is one of the seventy-two districts in the province of Ontario. YRDSB is a large, multicultural district just north of Toronto. It is a rapidly growing district with more than one hundred languages spoken in York schools. The board has been opening, on average, at least five new elementary schools a year for the last five years. There are a total of 170 schools in YRDSB, 140 elementary and 30 secondary schools.

We have been working in partnership since 2001 to improve literacy across the district. I will not get into details here (see Sharratt and Fullan, 2006), but in essence we have been putting into place the ten elements of successful change discussed in Chapter Three. York established a district plan called the Literacy Collaborative, which had five broad components:

1. A clearly articulated vision and commitment to a system literacy priority for all students that is constantly communicated to everyone in the system
2. A systemwide comprehensive plan and framework for continuous improvement
3. Using data to drive instruction and determine the resources
4. Building administration and teacher capacity to teach literacy to all students
5. Establishing professional learning communities at all levels of the system and beyond the district

It is a district with leaders who know the deep meaning of capacity building with a focus on results. School teams participate in continuous professional development to increase their content (in this case, literacy) expertise and their change knowledge as well as skills such as how to build professional learning communities. There is plenty of "learning in context" as principals and lead literacy teachers work with other teachers day in and day out. We deliberately use lateral capacity building to enable schools to learn from each other.

Over a three-year period, all schools (represented by teams) joined in the effort, going from 40 schools in September 2002 to 105 (2003) and all 170 schools (2004), including all 30 high schools that became involved because they wanted to work on literacy and develop other capacities.

There is a combination of a stay-the-course and an inquiry (evidence-based) mind-set that guides the initiative. For example, when the results for the seventeen most disadvantaged schools were not as impressive as district leaders thought they should be, given the investment, they took a closer look. It turned out that nine of the schools had focused thoroughly on implementing the literacy and change knowledge in the school compared to the other eight schools. When the two groups (these nine and the other eight) were compared, the differences were striking. At the beginning of the process, all seventeen schools were well below the York Region average in grade-three-ready scores. Four years later, the subgroup of nine more successful schools moved past the York average and well past the Ontario average.

The difference between the nine and the eight schools was not related to the attitude of school leaders to the initiative. All seventeen schools endorsed and committed to the project. School leaders in the nine successful cases, however, implemented the components of the reform more thoroughly; did continuous self-evaluation; and worked on aligning the beliefs and developing knowledge and skills among the principal, lead literacy teachers, special education resource teachers, and in turn the staff as a whole.

Four years later, York is reaping the benefits, with a substantial one-year increase (over 5 percent) in literacy scores across the board's 140 elementary schools. Still, it is time to dig deeper. For the 2005–06 school year, twenty-seven elementary and six secondary schools that were facing the greatest challenges and not getting satisfactory results were identified and are receiving additional school-based support focusing on approved student achievement in literacy. Each of these thirty-three schools will receive assistance from two curricular consultants and one curriculum coordinator who will work with the school leadership team to extend school-wide capacity for improved student achievement.

Concerning the evolution of positive pressure that I talked about in Chapter Three, the thirty-three schools have not been judged or made to feel inferior. The nonpejorative assumption was that more investment was needed in capacity building. Eventually, after all the excuses are off the table, judgment will be made relative to some situations, but it will come later in the process and be confined to a small number of cases. To speak more generally about turnaround schools, having a nonpejorative stance does not preclude that in some obvious cases a change in school leadership may be necessary up front.

In a sense one can consider the thirty-three schools as turn-around schools, but they are clearly part of an integrated districtwide development that applies to everyone. York schools are increasingly participating in action research grants the district provides for embedding improvement in schools, which involve self-reflection at the school and classroom level on "what works, what doesn't, and what can we do differently."

Transparency of results and access to each other's strategies and improvement plans has become a normal and comfortable characteristic of the district. In June of each year, all 170 schools present their accomplishments and acquired lessons at a learning fair for all to see.

Finally, York fits naturally into the Ontario-wide literacy strategy (which I turn to in a moment). For the 2005–06 year, the regional set of eleven districts (of which York is one) has received a grant from the province to learn from each other with respect to improving literacy achievement—cross-district lateral capacity development—in what amounts to regionwide literacy capacity building. District leaders increasingly endorse the idea that districts develop best in the long run if they learn from each other. It is the public system as a whole that must improve. These leaders take the intellectual (knowledge-based) and moral commitment (to a system beyond one's own) stance that it is their responsibility to learn from other districts and to contribute to the learning of other districts—the my-to-our mind-set shift we identified at the end of Chapter Three.

York is only one district among seventy-two in Ontario, albeit a large one. What about the system as a whole?

System Reform: The Ontario Case

We have England to thank for starting us down the path of whole system reform using a deliberate knowledge-based strategy. We had the privilege of evaluating England's National Literacy and Numeracy Strategy from 1999–2002 (Earl and others, 2003). In an impressive four years, literacy and mathematics achievement scores for eleven-year-olds moved from approximately 62 percent to 75 percent. I say impressive because we are talking about 150 local authorities (districts) and just under twenty thousand schools. There is some debate about whether the real gains were of that magnitude, but our evaluation certainly concluded that the gains were substantial and large scale.

The other side of the story is that the achievement plateaued in 2001 and remained at that level until recently. To use the terminology of this book, the plateau occurred because of the failure to mobilize a million change agents. It is instructive to note that after three years of flatlined results England has moved in the past two years (2004, 2005) from 75 percent to 80 percent using strategies proposed in this book, such as lateral capacity building in which schools are supported to learn from each other. In turnaround terms, England is getting good results in turning around failing secondary schools by federating them with successful schools (note there are many subtleties to how schools can best learn from each other, but the basic strategy is sound).

The good news is that we have the chance in Ontario to learn from the English experience, to design and carry out our own Ontario-based system reform. In April 2004 I was appointed by the premier of Ontario, Dalton McGuinty, as a special adviser to him and to the minister, Gerard Kennedy, and now-minister Sandra Pupatello. The task is to create a strategy that will substantially improve literacy and numeracy, within one election period so to speak, for all seventy-two school districts, all four thousand elementary schools in Ontario. We are attempting to do just that in all districts (twelve are francophone districts, twenty-eight Catholic, and thirty-two public, all fully publicly funded).

There are three main differences from the English strategy. First, the English strategy fixated on targets. The system was to move from 62 percent literacy in 1997 to 80 percent by 2002 (recall they reached 75 percent but now after shifting gears have arrived at 80 percent). After a famous meeting with all directors (superintendents) of education at the beginning of the process, each director was handed an envelope that contained the current literacy score in the district and a specified target for the next year; this was their centrally calculated share of getting to 80 percent.

Second, England has an inspection agency called the Office for Standards in Education (OFSTED), which in the early stages carried out a name-and-shame regime of identifying failing schools for immediate intrusive intervention (OFSTED currently has a more balanced approach).

Third, the literacy and numeracy curriculum and teaching practices to be followed were specified. Now called "informed prescription," the center worked on presenting what and how one should teach as part of the strategy.

My point here is not so much to judge the limitations of the English strategy but to stress the differences from the Ontario strategy. What I discuss in this section is our actual strategy, and the results we are getting so far. I offer the Ontario case not as an example to be copied but rather as a concrete case of what the full strategy looks like in actual practice.

The way to interpret the Ontario strategy and its components we are about to discuss is to think of them as a case-based manifestation of the ten elements of successful change that were examined in the latter part of Chapter Three. In other words, the theory of action underpinning the ten elements leads one to think about and do certain things arising from the elements. This is not blueprint time, because we are after all talking about complexity theory. But the fact is that more sophisticated theories are needed to go beyond turnaround schools, and such theories can be *practical;* they lead one to specific strategies that in turn can be applied, assessed according to ongoing evidence, and modified. Though the ten elements in Chapter Three are generic, any specific application will reflect local context. Hence our Ontario strategy is based on the ten elements but is crafted in more specific, context-based terms.

There are eight interlocking strategies that we are putting into place in Ontario. As I describe them briefly here, recall from Chapter Three that the main measure of an overall strategy is whether it is *motivational*, mobilizing a large number of people to put in their energy and otherwise invest in what will be required to reap and sustain major improvements. The key in large-scale reform is whether the strategy can get a large number of leaders (change agents) within and across the three levels to jointly own the enterprise. There are eight strategies:

1. A guiding coalition constantly in communication

2. Peace and stability and other "distractors"

3. The Literacy and Numeracy Secretariat

4. Negotiating aspirational targets

5. Capacity building in relation to the targets

6. Growing the financial investment

7. Evolving positive pressure

8. Connecting the dots with key complementary components

A Guiding Coalition

A Guiding Coalition is concerned with whether the small number of key leaders consistently communicate among themselves and with all other stakeholders, and further that they have the same message, which is capacity building with a focus on results through all eight strategic elements.

In Ontario's case, the Guiding Coalition includes the premier, the minister, the deputy minister (chief civil servant), the CEO of the secretariat, and me as special adviser, along with the relevant policy advisers. They need to meet often enough (in subgroups and as a whole) to continuously construct and agree on the nature of the strategy at work, problems being encountered, progress being made, and additional actions required. They also need to meet with constituent groups formally (which they do through partnership tables with all key groups—parents, teacher unions, administrator associates, school board trustees, and others) and informally through the many opportunities created by working with schools and districts in the course of implementing the other seven strategies. The Guiding Coalition must listen as well as promulgate the strategy.

A good hypothetical test of whether the coalition has its act together is to imagine that five newspaper reporters asked five members of the coalition the same question (such as, "What is the role of targets in your strategy?") on the same day and at the same time. The responses would be essentially consistent and specific across the five. Not only would they have a chance to check with each other, it would not occur to them that this would be necessary. This is not groupthink at work; the strategy is deeply understood (and in fine detail) as it is implemented and refined.

Peace and Stability

A deliberate part of our strategy is to address the distractors— anything that takes you away from continuous focus on teaching and learning and student achievement. A big distractor prior to 2003 was constant labor strife between unions and districts or government. Countless days and energy were lost to strikes and work-to-rule in the 1997–2002 period. Closing the gap is a system problem that needs a system solution, which you cannot reach if people are constantly sniping at each other.

To make an intense political story short, the minister of education, in partnership with unions and districts, created a framework to guide establishment of new collective bargaining agreements and then rode herd on completing agreements within a specified timeline. The result was that by June 2005 four-year agreements were signed encompassing all 122 collective agreements across the seventy-two districts—providing a significant period of potential labor stability, which I should add must not be taken as a given but pursued into implementation. For whole system reform, the energies of all parties must be devoted to addressing the core solutions of improving teaching, learning, and achievement. Labor-related distractions are especially debilitating. It is important to note that once the framework of collective agreements is agreed on, it is necessary to monitor implementation as new ideas and interpretations arise in the heat of everyday action. Hence we have established a Peace and Stability Commission, whose job it is to provide a normative framework and mechanism to resolve any problems between unions and management that surface during the course of everyday business.

We continue in the Ontario strategy to work to reduce or eliminate other distractors that take up time and energy at the expense of student learning. In our case these include reducing the amount of bureaucracy and unnecessary paperwork faced by districts and schools, simplifying a teacher appraisal scheme that consumes a large amount of principals' time without yielding positive results, and determining what can be done to help principals cope with the managerial side (budget, plant, and personnel) of their role so that they can devote time to the core work of building cultures that focus on learning and results. In short, if you are serious about closing the gap you have to make it possible to do so. Managing distractors is another of those issues that amount to taking excuses off the table.

The Literacy and Numeracy Secretariat

Ontario chose to focus on literacy and numeracy in order to establish foundational literacies. There is some work on what I referred to earlier as the third basic, well-being, but much more focus is necessary in the near future on this component. In the cognitive domain, it is not that other parts of the curriculum are unimportant but rather that literacy and numeracy are a special priority. They are pursued in their own right, and in relation to the rest of the curriculum.

Because capacity building (knowledge, resources, and motivation necessary to improve literacy ad numeracy) is a core part of our overall strategy, we created a brand new unit within the Ministry of

Education called the Literacy and Numeracy Secretariat. The CEO was hired from one of the seventy-two districts, where she was employed as director (superintendent) of education. The secretariat was established in 2004 and became fully staffed in 2005 with approximately sixty people. Most of the staff were hired from "the field," where they were leading literacy and numeracy superintendents, consultants, or other administrators. The goal was to create a new, innovative unit highly respected for its qualities by schools and districts that would work interactively with the latter in order to achieve results, especially concerning strategies four (aspirational targets) and five (capacity building).

The secretariat is organized into seven regional teams (about five to a team) who are responsible for working with the districts in a given region (we have already referred to the region in which York district is situated, which contains eleven large districts working together). In addition to the seven regional teams, there is a research team, an equity team, a capacity-building coordinating team, and an administrative support team.

The goals of the secretariat are to stimulate and sustain engagement across the province, to be responsive, and to initiate deeper strategies for reform. The secretariat is to be a proactive force to increase two-way development between districts and the government, and to stimulate lateral interaction across districts in seeking most effective practices.

Negotiating Aspirational Targets

Targets can be controversial. England's certainly were. As part of the election platform, Premier McGuinty, noting that Ontario's twelve-year-olds were scoring about 57 percent on literacy and numeracy in 2002 and were flatlined in previous years, announced a target of 75 percent for both literacy and numeracy by 2008. Incidentally, absolute scores should not be compared across countries (except if it is part of the same testing regimen, as with OECD's PISA program) because standards and cutoff points vary. Ontario has an independent assessment agency (Education Quality and Account-ability Office, or EQAO) that conducts annual assessments in literacy and numeracy at grades three and six. Ontario's standard of proficiency within its own assessment system is high, requiring substantial comprehension and performance in literacy and numeracy.

In any case, we entered the strategy with an overall target set at 75 percent. My colleagues, Hargreaves and Fink (2006), are against externally imposed targets, arguing that they are not owned and result in superficial actions and mistrust. Their argument seems to be around whether the targets are experienced as externally imposed; as they say, "People can and sometimes should set targets together as part of a shared commitment" (p. 48).

Our goal in Ontario is to negotiate targets with each of the seventy-two districts, not by handing them an envelope as the English did but by discussing starting points and negotiating next year's target as part of rolling reform. I have found that because these discussions occur within the context of the other seven strategy components they are nonproblematic. Most educators think that 75 percent as a five-year goal is reasonable for the province to aspire to; most think moving up 5 percentage points, say from 61 percent to 66 percent, is a desirable and achievable stretch for the next year, given the additional resources embedded in many of the elements of the strategy. Although I believe these directional goals and the strategy as a whole appear to be receiving widespread endorsement by educators, I am conscious of the fact that we are at the early stages of the initiative, and that we don't yet have full appreciation of the experiences of the everyday classroom teacher. As we proceed, the strategy needs (and will benefit from) a stronger infusion of teacher perspectives. We will attain this within the strategy, which involves a lot of two-way interaction with teachers, and through surveys and case studies. A basic premise of the overall strategy is to be evidence based, to learn as we go. Commitment to research and inquiry and timely action and correction are crucial to all large-scale change efforts.

Annual targets, in any case, are negotiated in interaction with the secretariat, the first ones for the end of school year 2004 and so on. We are careful not to detach targets from other key components such as capacity building. There is now engagement on the part of districts and schools to work on strategies in relation to literacy and numeracy, and excitement to see how they do when EQAO results are released. If you were to ask the seventy-two directors of education and the four thousand school principals whether they feel the targets are jointly owned, I believe that the vast majority would say yes. Again, the everyday teacher's voice must be incorporated here. We are not fixated on the target, but it is serious work with great moral purpose—for example, to see fifteen hundred more children become more literate with each percentage point of improvement for twelve-year-olds (grade six).

Capacity Building

Capacity building, as we have seen in Chapter Three, is multifaceted because it involves everything you do that affects new knowledge, skills, and competencies; enhanced resources; and stronger commitments. These are the main capacity-building components in our case:

- Ongoing professional development for the staff of the secretariat. If they are going to help in capacity building, they have to engage in it themselves.
- Interacting with districts to strengthen the capacity-building improvement plans each district prepares in relation to aspirational targets. We have developed an eight-component rubric that can be used as a tool to assess the quality of improvement strategies. There is an emphasis on keeping paper to a minimum. The purpose is to increase reflective action—strategizing more than strategy.
- Identifying and sharing effective practices in relation to both content (literacy and numeracy instruction) and strategy (change strategies that increase quality and extent of implementation). Each

regional area receives money to engage in lateral learning and capacity building.

• Developing resource materials for targeted issues such as boys and literacy, English as a second language, special education, and Aboriginal students.

• Conducting case studies of districts that (1) seem to have good strategies and (2) get good results (see Campbell and Fullan, 2006). The research arm of the secretariat in partnership with selected districts has just completed case studies in eight districts representing the whole range of circumstances in the province (a multicultural, large urban district in the south; huge, dispersed geographical sprawl with a high Aboriginal population in the north; francophone district in the east; Catholic county district in the west; and so on). These case studies are fed back to districts so that all can learn and spawn cross-district visits and learning exchanges.

• Building up the capacity for "assessment literacy," which is our term to encompass both assessment for and assessment of literacy. We have invested heavily in developing the high-yield capacity of assessment for learning at the school and district levels (see also the discussion on the nature and use of a provincewide database under "Evolving Positive Pressure" below).

• Creating a system of lead literacy and lead numeracy teachers in all four thousand schools. Our research has found that "second change agents" (in addition to the principal) are crucial. They work inside the school with other teachers to demonstrate new techniques, offer instructional resources, and link to other teachers' classrooms in the school and in other schools. In the most disadvantaged schools, lead literacy teachers are released full-time to work across the school.

• Ongoing professional development in summers and evenings to constantly update teachers, with a growing emphasis on working with teams, and lending support to teachers so they can learn in context as they apply the ideas in their own schools.

• A turnaround school program. This is a small but important part of the overall strategy in which low-performing schools in highly challenging circumstances *voluntarily* join a program of intensive support and development, run by the Ministry of Education using external expert coaches to work with selected schools over a three-year period. Because the program is voluntary, there is less stigma attached to it (all schools in the province are implicated anyway in the overall strategy). The turnaround program was introduced by the previous government but was a detached, stand-alone initiative. We are now able to incorporate it with district work in the context of an integrated strategy. In addition to more than 100 schools in the turnaround program, we have just identified 307 schools across some twenty districts that are "underperforming" and require further capacity-building assistance.

• Reducing class size in the early years (up to grade three) to a limit of twenty (many classrooms had reached thirty-plus students). We have been careful to go about this not as an end in itself but as part of a strategy to improve instruction: reduce class size *and* teach differently to be more effective.

The very use of the term *capacity building* has made a big difference. The term is now used readily and easily by everyone from the premier to classroom teachers. Capacity building means something because there are so many concrete examples of it in practice. People know it and value it because they are experiencing it.

Growing the Financial Investment

Money is not the answer, but the Education Trust's report (2005) on the funding gap with which I started this chapter got it right in the conclusion: "It is unfortunate that the debate over education funding is dominated by extreme views—with some claiming that money doesn't matter at all and others claiming reforms are impossible without additional dollars. Neither argument makes sense but both postpone the day when we will give poor students of color the education they deserve and need" (p. 9).

Even though Ontario was in a serious budget deficit situation when the new government came into power, the premier made it clear that education and education spending were a priority. To make this point, in public speeches he frequently says that "if given the choice of spending my next dollar on health or on education, I will choose education every time." Funding, especially directed at capacity building, has increased substantially.

The budget for education in Ontario in 2002–03 (that is, prior to the new strategy) was $16.9 billion (all figures expressed in Canadian dollars). In the first three years of the new initiatives, the budget increased to more than $18.4 billion. Cumulative new expenditures represent an increase of $8.3 billion over this period, or expressed as an increase from the base, growth of some 17 percent over this period (with inflation accounting for only 7%).

Much of the new money is devoted to capacity building for all those in challenging circumstances receiving additional earmarked resources. All this as the government is working to reduce an overall budget deficit.

The logic and strategy of growing the financial investment goes like this. Invest substantially at the front end to get the process kickstarted and to show goodwill and seriousness of commitment. Make it a quid pro quo proposition. As the government does its part, it in effect asks the field to do its share (in partnership, as I have stressed) by using the money to focus on priorities and by leveraging it into additional investments of energy, skill development, and commitment. As results move upward, use the momentum to lever more dollars from the treasury and elsewhere. This year's gains chase next year's additional money. Don't make literal judgments year by year, because trends take time and must be judged over three-year cycles. As Kanter (2004) states, "winning streaks attract investments" (p. 341).

Need I say that the fundamental premise underlying the argument in this book of raise the bar and close the gap is that if done well these investments are financially lucrative for society. They produce direct economic development and benefits; they save money by reducing the bill in education with respect to later remedial costs for failing students, and by affecting costs related to crime, health, and other aspects of well-being.

Evolving Positive Pressure

Positive pressure is nonpejorative at the outset, treats people with respect and dignity, appreciates and is empathic to challenging circumstances, furnishes assistance and support in the form of resources and capacity building, helps take all of the excuses off the table, and then turns ugly (for emphasis only) in cases of persistent low performance.

There are, of course, situations so egregiously wrong that tough, decisive action must be taken right away. But for large-scale system change, you need to motivate a large number of people. Positive pressure is designed to do that. If resources are provided and excuses are eliminated one by one, persistent good performance is going to be noticed in another light. So are situations where things fail to improve despite new investments. Peers are more likely to think that maybe it is poor teaching and leadership, bad attitudes, low expectations, lack of care, and the like. Leaders will find it easier to have pointed discussions that most would find fair and reasonable.

Let me give an example of assessment both for and of learning, dealing with the online database we are just establishing. Using Statistics Canada data, we have grouped the 4,000 elementary schools into four bands according to the percentage of students living in low-income households, which we call the low-income cutoff point (LICO, introduced in Chapter Three). There are 1,552 schools in the 0–5 percent LICO category, 1,343 schools in the 6–15 percent LICO group, 581 at 16–24 percent LICO, and 497 schools with more than 25 percent of the students in low-income households. All 4,000 schools by name (and by a variety of indicators), along with their reading, writing, and math scores for grades three and six, are in the database. The system will soon be online for all to access.

In addition, schools are also classified according to whether they are extremely far from the provincial target, far from it, somewhat near, or above the target. The database tracks improvement or lack thereof, which we view over three-year cycles according to several categories of school expressed in terms of whether the school is high or low in performance, as well as whether it is declining, stagnant, or improving (in relation to the three-year trend). We have two basic ground rules annunciated by the premier and the minister: we will not condone so-called league tables (comparing apples with oranges); and we will not interpret achievement results on a single year basis, favoring three-year rolling averages in order to discern real value added differences.

Well, you get the picture, and you can see where we are going with positive pressure. System leaders, for example, could look at the 1,552 schools with few poverty households (no apparent excuses) and ask by name why the two hundred schools in that category are "extremely far" or "far" from the provincial target. What if many of these schools were clustered in certain districts? When you do fair comparisons, apples to apples, people can learn from others in similar circumstances, and if you don't do anything to improve your situation the pressure mounts.

This analysis has led us to identify low-performing schools according to their LICO comparators. In our most recent intensive strategy—called the Ontario Focused Intervention Partnership (note the emphases on focus and on partnership)—we have identified all low achieving schools across the four LICO categories. There are 367 schools across 58 districts that are in this low achieving grouping. We are now working in partnership with the districts and schools to furnish greater capacity-building support along with pressure to make gains in student achievement according to their own starting points, and the performance of their comparators.

As far as I know, we are the first to put the spotlight on the cruising schools as a group. This leads to focusing on advantaged schools that are doing especially well compared to their peers in order to learn valuable lessons from them; and inevitably on schools that, despite their initial advantage, are not showing commensurate performance, and then to probe why they are not on the move and what could be done to ignite the stagnant situations.

Reeves (2006) captures the array of situations when he identifies schools that have favorable circumstances but fail to take advantage of them, and those that face difficult challenges and are trying to do something about it. He calls the former group (high initial advantage) "lucky." These schools may take advantage of their initial good circumstances, or they may cruise along, resting on the laurels of the students they inherited—akin to the person who was born on third base and thought he had hit a triple.

In addition to system use of the data profile, we are heading toward making the database available for individual schools. An individual school, for example, could use the Schools Like Me option and find by name the (let's say) 168 schools with similar profiles—for example, the same LICO category, urban, above five hundred students—and see where they fit in achievement expecting to learn from those doing better.

I hope I have stressed enough times that none of this is literal. You do need to know your stuff. You do need to appreciate the dynamics of all eight strategies in action. In Ontario as a policy matter we have explicitly and categorically rejected using league tables ranking all schools; we have even convinced one of the major Toronto newspapers not to publish league tables even though the information is freely available. League tables represent negative, unhelpful pressure. You have to start with comparing apples to apples and then move to gap closing. We have also taken the policy position that interpreting any one year's results can be misleading (odd blips occur, impact of strategies takes time, and trends cannot be discerned); thus we treat only three-year rolling trends as legitimate.

In all of this, the goal at the end of the day is to establish the conditions for discussion about performance that would be seen as reasonable and fair—to be able to have telling and revealing discussions with certain principals, directors of education, and others. If the overall strategy fails to produce widespread improvement, these telling discussions turn to the minister and the special adviser, and from the public to the premier. Positive pressure all around is the way it should be for an agenda so crucial to society.

Finally, another face of positive pressure is to compare one's own progress on an ongoing basis according to national and international standards. As noted earlier, OECD conducts excellent assessments in literacy, math, and science with carefully developed instruments and protocols. As it progresses, Ontario will want to compare itself with the performance of Alberta, the leading province in Canada, and Finland, which has recently been leading the pack of the thirty-two OECD countries.

Connecting the Dots with Key Complementary Components

You cannot do everything at once, which is why we have prioritized literacy and numeracy as the first order of business. As you go, however, it is necessary to begin working on linking to other key components that surround literacy and numeracy. I have already mentioned well-being as an essential element of the initial three basics. Other main complementary components are high school reform, early childhood, teacher education, and leadership development.

High school reform is obviously important in its own right, but also important because you want to build on the new increases in literacy and numeracy at the elementary level, as we are doing in York Region.

In this third year of the literacy and numeracy strategy, additional strategies are being added to work on high school reform. At the provincial level, a goal has been set to cut the high school dropout rate in half, from 30 percent to 15 percent. Each district has been funded to appoint a "student success" educator, who works in the district to provide more targeted support to students on the verge of dropping out. Programs are being revamped for more options for students who may be less interested in a university track. All over the developed countries, secondary school reform has lagged behind and is now getting the attention it deserves as part of the reform package.

Early childhood programs are a natural ally for our three basics of literacy, numeracy, and well-being. Diagnostic and intervention programs are being put in place, for example, to assess four-year-olds prior to entry to school. Early childhood is finally getting some attention but needs to be more prominent, stronger, and more specific as an articulated link to success at the elementary level.

Teacher education is another underdeveloped part of the reform picture. In England the Teacher Training Agency has been successful in strengthening the focus on literacy and numeracy in initial education, and in attracting new people to the profession through incentives related to the profession as a whole and with respect to the supply of teachers for certain subject areas, as well as for geographical areas in the country. Ontario is now turning its attention to teacher education by way of new requirements and resources to support teachers in the induction period.

I am reminded of the finding by Susan Moore Johnson (2004) that one-to-one mentoring of beginning teachers had no positive impact in isolated school cultures, but had major benefits if it operated within a collaborative or professional learning community culture. The interactive effects are obvious. To further connect the dots, units on effective teaching practices in literacy and numeracy could be added to the professional development of all new elementary school teachers through the mentoring and induction process—especially powerful if done in conjunction with development of professional learning communities, as we are now doing.

Leadership development is most obviously the key. Many of our strategies are based on leaders developing other leaders so that there is a greater critical mass of distributed leaders in the first place and a built-in pipeline of future leaders. Something direct must be done about the principalship in which new expectations have been added for the principal as leader of leaders in improving learning and closing the gap, *without* taking away or extending support for the managerial and community relations side of the role. We have already referenced the Cross City Campaign for Urban School Reform (2005) case studies of Chicago, Milwaukee, and Seattle. There was a lot of money for professional development for principals, which they experienced, but nobody changed the role to make it happen back at the school. Principals thus were not able to influence the instructional practices within the school and classrooms. In Ontario we have just issued a discussion paper with the principals' associations to concentrate on the tasks of reducing the distractors, adding more support for management tasks; increasing the focus or development of collaborative school cultures; and increasing the expectation and means for principals to be system leaders, who learn from and contribute to other schools while contributing to and influencing system priorities. Similar developments even further along can be found in the new corporate plan for the National College for School Leadership in England (NCSL, 2005).

The eight strategic components are currently being coordinated and implemented in Ontario, and early results are promising. After only two years there is enormous goodwill, commitment, and excitement at all levels of the system. In terms of student achievement, if we take grade six reading for example (the pattern is essentially the same for grade six writing and math, and grade three reading, writing, and math), after being flatlined below 60 percent proficiency for five years prior to 2003–04, there was an increase of 3 percent in 2004–05 and a further 5 percent in 2005–06. In effect we are going from 56 percent to 63 percent in two years (with the 2004–05 increase the largest single year jump since EQAO began its assessments in 1997). Subanalyses also confirm that relevant gaps are closing slightly—such as between low- and high-performing districts, low- and high-performing schools, and boys and girls—as everyone moves up.

This is no time to claim success. We are aware of Kanter's law, that everything can look like a failure in the middle, or its corollary

"Early success is fragile"; small initial victories do not yet represent a trend. Much hard work remains, and it would not take many missteps for goodwill to dissipate. Will people be able to stay the course and develop greater capacity as the problems become harder? The external confidence of parents, the community, business leaders, and the media may have increased slightly, but it remains tentative. Teacher unions are still wary after years of conflict with the previous government and are tentatively supporting the direction (whereas going the distance requires strong teacher union leadership). We also need to look for other jurisdictions where strong successful partnerships are developing with teacher unions. Teacher unions as well as governments have their work cut out in gaining public confidence, and it is in their best interests to partner in the agenda laid out in this book.

The whole arena of public confidence, as Kanter notes, is essential to sustaining a winning streak. There are few winning streaks as crucial to society as establishing momentum for people to invest their energies and resources in raising the bar and reducing the income and education gap in society.

Ontario is a work in progress, but it represents a good example in which we are trying to combine all our knowledge of change to bring about reform in the system as a whole—to raise the bar and close the gap in literacy and numeracy. It is an example of trying to learn from others as we contribute our lessons learned to the global community of system reformers. It is time to dramatically and explicitly increase our mutual efforts within and across countries to directly tackle what I have called the real reform agenda.

Radical experiments are now surfacing in many places; policymakers know that virtually all strategies have failed over the past decades to achieve needed breakthroughs. Centralized high-stakes accountability schemes have failed to produce ownership, as has decentralized site-based management.

The solution, in my view, is to develop strategies that integrate top-down and bottom-up forces in an ongoing, dynamic manner,

achieving what I call "permeable connectivity." We saw one version of this in the Ontario case just presented. England is attempting to move in this direction with its Every Child Matters agenda.
In rebuilding New Orleans after Katrina, Louisiana is exploring how
it can make a fresh start, avoid the previous dysfunctionality of its
local school board, and move toward empowering and mobilizing
community and school forces. Indeed, Katrina has posed this challenge for revamping Louisiana as a whole state. New York City also
presents a case study of running the gamut of solutions, moving over
the past decade from thirty-two subdistricts to ten instructional
regions and in its most recent move to establish "autonomous zones"
intended to give power and resources to schools to act within a
district and state framework. There is currently a pilot group of 42
such schools with plans to expand to 150 more schools in the fall
of 2006.

The word *autonomy* would not get at the solution envisaged in
this book. Permeable connectivity requires a sophisticated and delicate balance, because to work it requires all three levels—school,
community and district, and state—to interact regularly across and
within levels. We don't want the inadequacies of tightly controlled
centralization being replaced with the equal flaws of school and
community autonomy. The answer, so to speak, is to have state
interests present in local settings, while local interests are reflected
in state thinking and action. Instead of local autonomy, we need
clusters of schools engaged in lateral capacity building, incorporat-
ing state and local agendas. Clustering of networks of schools is
essential to the future because it compensates for the dangers of isolated autonomy without succumbing to top-down running of
schools. The Ontario case represents some aspects of this model,
although likely not the full solution that should evolve in the next
stages of reform. In any case, we are entering an exciting period
because people at all levels of the system are willing to try breakthrough ideas; we have exhausted the capacity of existing strategies.

Coda

Four chapters: the real reform, turnaround schools, change, and system. One unified agenda: to turn a system around by substantially raising the bar and closing the gap in educational performance, while realizing that this is part of a larger goal to reduce the income differential in society as whole. As Wilkinson (2005) says, the alternative to destructive pursuit of higher levels of consumption is not stagnation but "a process of social and technical innovation to serve social and environmental purposes" (p. 315).

Kanter's winning streaks are not created by single leaders getting ahead of the pack, but instead by combining accountability, collaboration, and initiative. The combination produces a lot of powerful innovation, more broadly endorsed and used.

All of this is to say that the quality of life that we all seek depends primarily on the nature of the social environment. People will be motivated to improve rather than reduce the quality of the social environment when "personal interactions make people feel valued and appreciated, rather that put down and ignored" (Wilkinson, p. 316). Social environments need to be changed to bring out the best in people, not to remain as they are now in many situations that, in effect, continue to give excuses and in some ways an irresistible psychological urge to engage in antisocial and destructive behavior.

Why not use our human and social ingenuity to mobilize the million change agents that it will take to accomplish two giant things at once: greater equality and multifaceted prosperity? This is education's true calling in the twenty-first century. It is time to go far beyond turnaround schools and to tackle head-on the deep system transformation called for in order to reduce income and education gaps. The stakes have never been higher.

References

Ansell, D. *Improving Schools Facing Challenging Circumstances*. Nottingham, England: National College for School Leadership, 2004.

Barber, M., and Fullan, M. "Tri-Level Development: It's the System." *Education Week*, Mar. 2, 2005, pp. 15–16.

Bate, P., Bevan, H., and Robert, G. *Towards a Million Change Agents: A Review of the Social Movements Literature*. London: National Health System, 2005.

Berliner, D. "Our Impoverished View of Education Reform." *Teachers College Record*, August 2005, pp. 1–36.

Berwick, D. "Improvement, Trust, and Healthcare Workforce." *Quality and Safety in Health Care*, 2003, *12*(6), 448–452.

Bryk, A., and Schneider, B. *Trust in Schools*. New York: Russell Sage, 2002.

Campbell, C., and Fullan, M. "Unlocking the Potential for District Wide Reform." (Unpublished paper.) Toronto: Literacy and Numeracy Secretariat, Ontario Ministry of Education, 2006.

Campbell, E. *The Ethical Teacher*. Philadelphia: Open University Press, 2003.

Campbell, E. "Challenges in Fostering Ethical Knowledge as Professionalism Within Schools as Teaching Communities." *Journal of Educational Change*, 2005, *6*(3), 207–226.

Coulombe, S., and Tremblay, J. F. *Public Investment in Skills*. Toronto: C. D. Howe Institute, 2005.

Cross City Campaign for Urban School Reform. *A Delicate Balance: District Policies and Classroom Practice*. Chicago: Cross City Campaign for Urban Reform, 2005.

Deutschman, A. "Change or Die." *Fast Company*, May 2005, *94*, pp. 53–57.

DuFour, R., Eaker, R., and DuFour, R. (eds.). *On Common Ground*. Bloomington, Ind.: National Education Services, 2005.

Earl, L., Fullan, M., Leithwood, K., and Watson, N. *Watching and Learning: OISE/UT Evaluation of the National Literacy and Numeracy Strategies*. London: Department for Education and Skills, 2003.

Education Trust. *The Funding Gap 2005: Low-Income and Minority Students Shortchanged by Most States*. Washington, D.C.: Education Trust, 2005.

Elmore, R. "The Hollow Core of Leadership Practice in Education." (Unpublished paper.) Harvard University Graduate School of Education, 2004a.

Elmore, R. *School Reform from Inside out*. Cambridge: Harvard Education Press, 2004b.

Frank, R. H. *Luxury Fever: Why Money Fails to Satisfy in an Era of Success*. New York: Free Press, 1999.

Fullan, M. *Change Forces with a Vengeance*. London: Falmer Press, 2003.

Fullan, M. *Leadership and Sustainability*. Thousand Oaks, Calif.: Corwin Press; Toronto: Ontario Principal's Council, 2005.

Fullan, M., Hill, P., and Crévola, C. *Breakthrough*. Thousand Oaks, Calif.: Corwin Press; Toronto: Ontario Principal's Council, 2006.

Fullan, M., and St. Germain, C. *Learning Places*. Thousand Oaks, Calif.: Corwin press; Toronto: Ontario Principal's Council, 2006.

Gardner, H. *Changing Minds*. Boston: Harvard Business School Press, 2004.

Gilligan, J. *Violence: Our Deadly Epidemic and Its Causes*. New York: Putnam, 1996.

Gordon, M. *Roots of Empathy: Changing the World Child by Child*. Toronto: Thomas Allen, 2005.

Hargreaves, A. *Teaching and the Knowledge Society*. New York: Teachers College Press, 2003.

Hargreaves, A. "Distinction and Disgust: The Emotional Politics of School Failure." *International Journal of Leadership in Education*, 2004, 7(1), 27–41.

Hargreaves, A., and Fink, D. *Sustainable Leadership*. San Francisco: Jossey-Bass, 2006.

Heckman, J. "Investing in Disadvantaged Children Is an Economically Efficient Policy." Paper presented at Committee for Economic Development Forum on Building the Economic Case for Investments in Preschool, New York, Jan. 10, 2006.

Herszenhorn, D. "New York Rethinks Its Remaking of the Schools." *Sunday New York Times*, Apr. 9, 2006.

Johnson, S. M. *Finders and Keepers: Helping New Teachers Thrive and Survive in Our Schools*. San Francisco: Jossey-Bass, 2004.

Kanter, R. M. *Confidence: How Winning and Losing Streaks Begin and End*. New York: Crown Business, 2004.

Leithwood, K. *Teacher Working Conditions That Matter.* Toronto: Elementary Teachers Federation of Ontario, 2005.

Levin, J., Mulhern, J., and Schunck, J. *Unintended Consequences: The Case for Reforming the Staffing Rules in Urban Teachers Union Contracts.* New York: New Teacher Project, 2005.

Marion, R. *The Edge of Organization.* Thousand Oaks, Calif.: Sage, 1999.

Minthrop, H. *Schools on Probation.* New York: Teachers College Press, 2004.

National Audit Office. *Improving Poorly Performing Schools in England.* London: Department for Education Skills, 2006.

National College for School Leadership. *Charting a Course.* Nottingham, England: National College of School Leadership, 2005.

Nye, B., Konstantopoulos, S., and Hedges, L. "How Large Are Teacher Effects?" *Educational Evaluation and Policy Analysis,* 2004, *26,* 237–257.

Oakes, J., and Lipton, J. "Struggling for Educational Equity in Diverse Communities: School Reform as Social Movement." *Journal of Education Change,* 2002, *3*(3–4), 383–406.

Ontario Ministry of Education. *The Literacy and Numeracy Secretariat, EQAO Analysis.* Toronto: Ontario Ministry of Education, 2005.

Organization for Economic Cooperation and Development (OECD). *Knowledge and Skills for Life: First Results from PISA 2000.* Paris: OECD, 2003.

Pervin, B. "Turning Around Student Achievement in Literacy." *Orbit,* 2005, *35*(2), 39–40.

Pfeffer, J., and Sutton, R. *The Knowing-Doing Gap.* Boston: Harvard Business School Press, 2000.

Reeves, D. *The Learning Leader.* Alexandria, Va.: Association for Supervision and Curriculum Development, 2006.

Rothstein, R. *Out of Balance.* (30th anniversary essay.) Chicago: Spencer Foundation, 2002.

Rothstein, R. *Class and Schools: Using Social, Economic, and Education Reform to Close the Black-White Achievement Gap.* Washington, D.C.: Economic Policy Institute, 2004.

Rudduck, J., Chaplain, R., and Wallace, G. *School Improvement: What Pupils Can Tell Us.* London: David Fulton, 1996.

Schmidt, J. "Congress Utterly Fails in Its Commitment to America's Schoolchildren." (Press release.) Washington, D.C.: National School Boards Association, 2005.

Sennett, R., and Cobb, J. *The Hidden Injuries of Class.* New York: Knopf, 1973.

Sharratt, L., and Fullan, M. "The School District That Did the Right Things Right." *Journal of School Leadership,* May 2006.

Stoll, L., and Fink, D. "The Cruising School: The Identified Ineffective School."
    In L. Stoll and K. Meyers (eds.), *No Quick Fixes*. London: Falmer
    Press, 1998.

Surowiecki, J. *The Wisdom of Crowds*. New York: Doubleday, 2004.

Wheatley, M. *Finding Our Way: Leadership for an Uncertain Time*. San Francisco:
    Berrett-Koehler, 2005.

Wilkinson, R. *The Impact of Inequality*. London: New Press, 2005.

Willms, J. D. (ed.). *Vulnerable Children: Findings from a Longitudinal Study of
    Children and Youth*. Edmonton: University of Alberta Press, 2003.

Index

vulnerability study findings on SES and, 10–12. *See also* Students

Class size, 87

Classrooms: black box of instructional practice in, 72–73; practice change in, 57–58. *See also* Schools

Cluster-based strategy, 58

Cobb, J., 23, 24

Collaboration strategy, 31–32, 58

Collective action mobilization, 40–41

Collective responsibility, 26

Collective wisdom, 38–39

Complexity (or chaos) theory, 37–38

Confidence: How Winning and Losing Streaks Begin and End (Kanter), 25

Confidence: actions for restoring, 54–55; building public, 64–67; external, 65; restoring people's, 54–60

Confidence issue, 25

"Congress Utterly Fails in Its Commitment to America's Schoolchildren" (Schmidt), 70

Cost issues. *See* Expenditure gap

Coulombe, S., 7

Crévola, C., 47, 58

Cross City Campaign for Urban School Reform, 56–57, 71–73, 94

Curriculum: character education, 46; emotional

intelligence, 46; "informed prescription," 79; safe schools, 46; three basics, 46–48

D

"Dangers of false recovery," 26

Deutschman, A., 35, 36, 55

Developed-underdeveloped country gap, 2–10

Dignity, 48–52

Discontinuity planning, 29, 30–31

Discrimination: downward, 49–50; societal inequalities and, 5

Disrespect, 48–49

"Distinction and Disgust: The Emotional Politics of School Failure" (Hargreaves), 23

Distractor management, 81–82

"Documentarianism" disease, 59

Double jeopardy hypothesis, 11–12

Downward discrimination, 49–50

E

Earl, L., 77

Education levels: benefits of closing gap in, 8–9, 15; labor productivity related to, 7

Education Quality and Accountability Office (EQAO) [Ontario], 84, 85, 94

Education systems: closing the gap in, 8–9, 15; examining consequences of inequality

TITLES IN THE JOSSEY-BASS
LEADERSHIP LIBRARY IN EDUCATION SERIES

Ann Lieberman, Lynne Miller
Teacher Leadership

Teacher Leadership is written for teachers who assume responsibility for educational success beyond their own classrooms by providing peer support, modeling good practice, or coordinating curriculum and instruction. It offers cases studies of innovative programs and stories of individual teachers who lead in a variety of contexts. It shows how to develop learning communities that include rather than exclude, create knowledge rather than merely applying it, and provide challenge and support to new and experienced teachers.

ISBN 0-7879-6245-7   Paperback   112 Pages   2004

Robert J. Starratt
Ethical Leadership

In *Ethical Leadership*, Robert Starratt—one of the leading thinkers on the topic of ethics and education—shows educational leaders how to move beyond mere technical efficiency in the delivery and performance of learning. He explains that leadership requires a moral commitment to high quality learning, based on three essential virtues: proactive responsibility, personal and professional authenticity, and an affirming, critical, and enabling presence. He challenges educators to become ethical leaders who understand the learning process as a profoundly moral activity that engages the full humanity of the school community.

ISBN 0-7879-6564-2   Paperback   176 Pages   2004

James Ryan
Inclusive Leadership

This is an innovative and groundbreaking book about the powerful new idea of inclusive leadership. The culture of schools and the diversity of those who lead them have not kept pace with the growing diversity in the student population. Counteracting the pernicious and pervasive processes of exclusion in our schools, James Ryan looks upon leadership as a collective influence process to promote inclusion. His work focuses on leadership as an intentionally inclusive practice that values all cultures and types of students and educators in a school. In four chapters, Ryan provides an overview of the topic, a summary of research, examples of good practice, and guidelines for the future.

ISBN 0-7879-6508-1   Paperback   192 Pages   2005

Andy Hargreaves and Dean Fink
Sustainable Leadership

This book addresses one of the most important and often neglected aspects of leadership: sustainability. The authors set out a compelling and original framework of seven principles for sustainable leadership characterized by Depth of learning and real achievement rather than superficially tested performance; Length of impact over the long haul, beyond individual leaders, through effectively managed succession; Breadth of influence, where leadership becomes a distributed responsibility; Justice in ensuring that leadership actions do no harm to and actively benefit students in other schools; Diversity that replaces standardization and alignment with diversity and cohesion; Resourcefulness that conserves and renews leaders' energy and doesn't burn them out; and Conservation that builds on the best of the past to create an even better future.

ISBN 0-7879-6838-2   Paperback   352 Pages   2005

James Spillane
Distributed Leadership

Distributed Leadership explores how leadership happens in everyday practices in schools, through formal routines and informal interactions. Spillane examines the distribution of leadership among administrators, specialists, and teachers in the school, and explains the ways in which leadership practice is stretched over leaders, followers, and aspects of the situation, including routines and tools of various sorts in the organization such as memos, scheduling procedures, and evaluation protocols. The book provides an overview of what it means to take a distributed perspective on leadership, an examination of various uses of the term, a summary of the most current research, illustrative examples, and helpful guidelines.

ISBN 0-7879-6538-3   Paperback   144 Pages   2006

Thomas Payzant and Janice E. Jackson
Urban School Leadership

ISBN 0-7879-8621-6   Paperback   144 Pages (approx.)   Fall 2007

OTHER BOOKS BY MICHAEL FULLAN

Leading in a Culture of Change

"At the very time the need for effective leadership is reaching critical proportions, Michael Fullan's *Leading in a Culture of Change* provides powerful insights for moving forward. We look forward to sharing it with our grantees.'
—*Tom Vander Ark, executive director, Education, Bill and Melinda Gates Foundation*

"Fullan articulates clearly the core values and practices of leadership required at all levels of the organization. Using specific examples, he convinces us that the key change principles are equally critical for leadership in business and education organizations."
—*John Evans, chairman, Torstar Corporation*

"In *Leading in a Culture of Change*, Michael Fullan deftly combines his expertise in school reform with the latest insights in organizational change and leadership. The result is a compelling and insightful exposition on how leaders in any setting can bring about lasting, positive, systemic change in their organizations."
—*John Alexander, president, Center for Creative Leadership*

"Michael Fullan's work is remarkable. He masterfully captures how leaders can significantly improve their learning and performance, even in the uncontrollable, chaotic circumstances in which they practice. A tour de force."
—*Anthony Alvarado, chancellor of instruction, San Diego City Schools*

Business, education, and public sector leaders are facing new and daunting challenges—rapid-paced developments in technology, sudden shifts in the marketplace, and crisis and contention in the public arena. If they are to survive in this chaotic environment, leaders must develop the skills they need to lead effectively no matter how fast the world around them is changing.

Leading in a Culture of Change offers new and seasoned leaders insights into the dynamics of change and presents a unique and imaginative approach for navigating the intricacies of the change process. Michael Fullan shows how leaders in all types of organizations can accomplish their goals and become exceptional leaders. He draws on the most current ideas and theories on the topic of effective leadership, incorporates case examples of large scale transformation, and reveals a remarkable convergence of five core competencies:

attending to a broader moral purpose, keeping on top of the change process, cultivating relationships, sharing knowledge, and setting a vision and context for creating coherence in organizations.

ISBN 0-7879-8766-2   Paperback   161 Pages

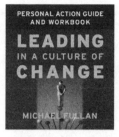

Leading in a Culture of Change
Personal Action Guide and Workbook

Change is an inevitable part of today's organizational life. To survive as a leader you must develop the skills that will mobilize your constituents to do important work no matter how fast the world around you is changing.

Leading in a Culture of Change Personal Action Guide and Workbook is an essential companion to Michael Fullan's bestselling book, *Leading in a Culture of Change*. This practical guide is designed to help leaders in all sectors (corporate, education, public, and nonprofit) manage and drive productive change within their organizations.

The workbook is filled with illustrative case examples, exercises, and resources that you can use with individuals or groups. It will help you (and any change agent) integrate the five core competencies—attending to a broader moral purpose, keeping on top of the change process, cultivating relationships, sharing knowledge, and setting a vision and context for creating coherence in organizations—and empower you to deal with the issues of complex change.

Leading in a Culture of Change Personal Action Guide and Workbook includes

- Practical tools—cases, activities, action steps, resources—that all go a long way to helping leaders implement change in organizations
- Questions that stimulate the application of concepts, techniques, and possibilities
- Summaries of key points, personal assessment exercises, and discussion points
- An easy-to-use format that has plenty of space for notes and lies flat for photocopying

Once you have worked through this book you will have developed a deep understanding that will be a benefit to you personally and professionally.

ISBN: 0-7879-6969-9   Paperback   272 pages